# The Tall Poppy

# The Tall Poppy

*How to grow to your full potential...*
*and keep your head*

*by*

*Judi James and Mike Edden*

First published in 1999 by
The Industrial Society
Robert Hyde House
48 Bryanston Square
London W1H 2EA    Telephone: 020 7479 2000

© The Industrial Society 1999
Reprinted June 2001

ISBN 1 85835 514 1
Ref: 1600tw 5.01

The Industrial Society USA
163 Central Avenue, Suite 2
Dover, NH 03820, USA

**British Library Cataloguing-in-Publication Data.**
**A catalogue record for this book is available from the**
**British Library.**

**Library of Congress**
**Cataloging-in-Publication**
**Data on File.**

Typeset by: The Midlands Book Typesetting Company
Printed by: J.W. Arrowsmith Ltd
Cover by: Sign Design
Cover image: Photonica

The Industrial Society is a Registered Charity No. 290003

# Acknowledgements

With thanks to Morgan Edden, whose keyboard and artistic skills helped create 'this book.

To all the people who took the time to share their ideas and quotes with us.

# Contents

# Introduction

> 'Some people dream of great achievements, others stay awake and make them happen.' **Anon**

This book will not intellectualise, dramatise, or over-excite. Its power lies in the simplicity and honesty of its messages. You can use it as a workbook for personal goal-achievement. Its aim is to inspire, educate and entertain, underpinning the levels of positive thinking and self-motivation needed to succeed in any or every aspect of your life.

## Why the tall poppy?

As co-authors of this book our backgrounds could hardly be more different: one a qualified engineer with industrial managerial experience, the other from the world of fashion, PR, journalism and marketing.

What we both recognised, however, whilst working together running training programmes for leading businesses, was that people who had achieved a high level of success in terms of wealth and/or status often appeared to be miserable or uncomfortable with their achievements. The idea that success naturally brings happiness in its wake is a myth. Grow in stature in terms of income and rank and you may find others start gunning for you. Or you may find yourself beginning to press the button marked 'self destruct'. The Tall Poppy syndrome describes this condition perfectly: nurture the plant until it grows higher than the others, and then lop off its head!

The list of high profile tall poppies grows every day in the press, as famous faces in sport, politics, business and the media appear hell-bent on scuppering their hard-won achievements with behaviour that borders on the bizarre and incomprehensible.

'I made an error of judgement' they exclaim, which just has to beggar the question: Why? Why would someone capable of such good judgement and career dedication suddenly choose to act in such a self-destructive manner? Why spoil all that you have achieved? And why does watching this very public fall from grace give the rest of us so much enjoyment?

For every tall poppy capable of acts of gross stupidity there are legions of people waiting in the sidelines, secateurs at the ready, pruning and dead-heading before the flower has even shown signs of wilting...

The good news, however, is it doesn't have to be this way. You can become a tall poppy – growing to your full potential – without losing your head! There will be risks, but there are as many risks if you don't make a move. Put simply, you have three options:

1. Don't bother.
   Achieve nothing and no-one can cut you down to size.
2. Emulate self-destructive tall poppies.
   Scupper your own achievements.
3. Control your own success.

Plan your objectives and strategies carefully. Be the tall poppy that keeps its head.

This is exactly what this book will help you to do. By working out goals (both large and small) that are specific to you, and you alone, you will be starting to grow – you will be taking your first steps along the route to success. Having done this, the book will help you work on all the skills that are vital to achieving this chosen success. Identifying pitfalls and barriers and building strategies to deal with them will be your next step.

Finally, you will move on to the chapter entitled The Slope of Achievement.

The Slope is the diagram you will find on p.155. It represents your path to achieving your objectives. This is followed by some short self-analysis tables which will help you clarify just what is involved on your particular journey.

## Like a poppy, you will be growing along the way

### Self-discovery

You can use this book to avoid those two sad realisations that people normally only discover when it is too late:

1. I never tried or did anything with my life.
2. I clawed my way to the top, making sacrifices along the way, only to find I'd focused on the wrong objective all along.

This book will unlock your potential by enabling you to set and challenge personal goals, and then discover and mine the motivation, mindsets and strategies necessary to realise your core ambitions. Its scope is holistic. The initial vision comes from within you. Its spirit comes from a sense of self-discovery.

The hardest step you will take with this book is to find out where you want to get to. Blurred vision is the greatest obstacle to your success. Knowing what you *don't* want is always easier than discovering what you do.

Once your goal is firmly in sight, however, your route will become less complicated to chart.

This emphasis on objective-focus has led to links being forged between business and sporting success. Create the vision and then build the stamina and motivation to achieve it. The comparison is obvious, and useful. What is equally obvious, though, is that winning in sport is rarely the same as winning in business, where goals are less defined or simple and set-backs far more subtle.

Success in sport can be instantaneous and transitory. As John Gorman, ex-assistant England football coach says, 'One goal and your whole career changes.'

Another example is mountaineering. A climber's goal is simple – to reach the peak. The minute he or she starts planning and then climbing that will be the sole focus of achievement. Grapple your way to the top, stick a flag in, take a breather, have a look around and admire the view and – as long as you get down again in one piece – you can pretty much call yourself successful.

Real life is rarely that clean cut, though. Getting a ball into a net, or getting to the tape before the other runners do – the very defined and simplistic nature of these goals makes the physical and mental preparation easier to plan. We know that real life is a lot more complex, which is why this book takes an altogether more flexible and realistic approach to challenging and then achieving your goals.

And what about that advice from leading entrepreneurs, telling you how to get rich quick or rise to the top in your chosen career? Great stuff, but does it help you with the smaller achievements? What if your idea of success is giving up work and retiring to a desert island?

For the purposes of this book, it is vital that you decide the size and scope of your objectives.

Current business culture has created a corporate society where 'high-income, high-achievement' is the standard criterion for success. And yet contentment and happiness are achieved at different levels, once the guilt of low achievement has been pared away.

You can use this book to change and improve your career or situation, but you can also use it to confirm any suspicions that you may be happier staying just the way you are.

Anyone can share the vision of getting first past the winning post, but your goals for the purpose of this book are going to be accountable to you and you alone. If you pause half way up the Slope of Achievement and decide you like the current reality there so much you want to stop, then you will have achieved your objective, and that's great. Success doesn't come from following other people's dreams, only your own.

## The scope of your dreams

Don't worry if your objectives are small. The size of your dream doesn't matter. The strategies we'll be showing you will be effective whatever your goals. You could use them to help you make your first million, or you could use them to help you move house, learn a new skill, even to lose a couple of pounds in weight.

## Scoring an own goal

Happiness is not prescriptive and yours may come cheaper than you expect. Top jobs and top incomes are no guarantee of contentment or satisfaction, which is why those high-achievers we met were made miserable by their own success. QUITE SIMPLY THEY HAD PURSUED THE WRONG GOAL.

You need to become obsessed with the day-to-day reality of your vision, whatever its scope. What you want to become may be a world apart from what you want to be doing.

## The effort-free guide

Honesty is not the greatest marketer of self-help manuals, which is why 'The Long Hard Grind to Wealth and Success' has yet to be written, while a flotilla of 'Two-minute Guides to Making a Million and being Immensely Popular without Lifting a Finger' is launched into the bookshops every year. You may have a shelf-full already. If your problem is how to get great wealth for no effort then the answer is easy:

1. Buy a lottery ticket.
2. Cross your fingers and keep them crossed for a very long time, probably forever.

Sorry, but you knew that was the reality, didn't you? You just hoped someone would tell you otherwise.

The only other route to effort-free money is to be heir to a fortune, but born-into-wealth people don't – as a rule – go around reading self-help manuals, so it's a pretty safe assumption you don't fall into that category!

## Laziness may suit you

Acknowledging current contentment with your lot is no more a crime than over-ambition. Understanding and then achieving or obtaining what you need to make you happy is the simple formula for success, but those needs will be as individual to you as your DNA. Motivation and self-awareness are the two main factors that will help create that happiness.

## Rule number 1

To repeat: don't allow anyone else to set your objectives. That has to be done by you.

## Success scares us

Failure can hurt, but it keeps us well within our comfort zone. Failure brings support, sympathy, empathy, caring and friendship. Success, on the other hand, can lead to envy and distancing. Success may also bring discomfort. Yet we spend most of our lives seeking comfort.

Try a simple experiment. Fold your arms. Which arm is on top? This is the way you always cross your arms. It is a learned habit. It feels comfortable because it is what you always do. Now cross them so that the other arm is on top. How does that feel? Uncomfortable? What do you want to do next? Re-fold your arms the usual way and return to that feeling of comfort?

Very few people succeed in life by staying inside their comfort zone. To succeed you are going to have to move forward through discomfort.

What scares us most is not our own inadequacies. Many people are comfortable with losing and being miserable, even though they don't like it. It's within their scope of experience. They can deal with it because they're used to it. It feels OK because it feels familiar. It's also the easier option. It brings no life change, no decisions and no unexpected situations. They're also happy moaning. It's a passive response to not getting what you want. It requires little action.

What terrifies us deep down inside is the scope of our own potential: what we could achieve if we stopped whinging and went out and made some changes – how much we are capable of and what heights we could climb.

The Tall Poppy syndrome – whereby we scupper our own success – is not a uniquely British phenomenon, but it is one that is rife in the culture of this country.

What makes us relish others' downfall? Jealousy, maybe? Yet their successes should be inspirational, not envy-inducing. Do they make us feel guilty because we haven't tried hard enough? Do we dislike the constant reminder of what we could have achieved if we'd bothered? Does their subsequent tumble from popularity and/or power reinforce our belief that it's really not worth all the effort in the first place? Or do we just like a good old laugh at the sight of pride and pomposity coming unstuck?

So what about all those celebrities who pack the drying out clinics for drink or drug addictions? And how about the political figures who get caught out on sexual or financial shenanigans?

If their sole focus was to succeed in their chosen careers wouldn't they have passed on the booze and bawdy romps? Blame the press, blame the pressures of the job, blame your parents, but ultimately we are all in charge of our own behaviour.

Why do we have so much trouble feeling comfortable with success; either our own or others? What makes the British in particular enjoy failure so much that we are happy to be a nation of 'also rans' in the sporting, performing and business fields? Why are we so good at mentally scuppering our own achievement before it has even reached lift-off? Why confuse confidence with arrogance and self-belief with inflated ego? And – most importantly – how can we overcome all this barriered thinking?

## National diffidence

No-one likes genuine arrogance, smugness or boastfulness, but as a nation the British suffer from a surfeit of self-effacing modesty. We reward the tryers and distrust the winners. Our hearts go out to the also-rans while the only ones who stay the course and maintain our affection and admiration are those who appear to have done so by accident or fluke.

You have a choice, then. Do you want to be another victim of Tall Poppy syndrome, nurturing your own success and then scuppering it at the last minute, either because you couldn't stand the pressure, or because you found yourself unhappy or lacking in commitment? Or do you want to be the tall poppy that grows to its full potential… and keeps its head?

Do you want to plot your route to individual achievement carefully, so that each step on the way is sound and potential set-backs well planned for? Do you want to target the right objectives, or just snatch at any goals that happen to take your fancy, regardless of their suitability to your personality or lifestyle? Do you need to know what will make you happy or can you just guess? And don't you think you should look at the whole picture before you start out en route to success? Shouldn't you balance commitments, ambitions and stages of change, as well as emotional and physical factors before you embark?

**Of course you should.**
And this book will help you do it.

Positive mindsets are vital, but not enough. Hard work and planning will be necessary too. So read on…

# CHAPTER 1

# A dreamer's guide – why millionaires and managers look so miserable

> 'My motivation comes from my love for the game and getting paid for doing something I enjoy. You have to stay positive and accept the defeat as part of football and take it as it comes. You can enjoy and get used to the uncertainty of the game.'
>
> **John Gorman, previous Assistant Coach to the England football team, currently coach at Ipswich Town football club**

It is essential for the purposes of your success plan that you draw a clear distinction between dreams and goals.

Daydreams are a crucial part of your mental well-being. Children daydream and it helps fuel their creativity. The edges between reality and dream-life were less distinct when you were a child. This aided your development as your self-perceived boundaries for potential achievement were virtually non-existent. You dismissed less because you dreamt more.

## Obscured by clouds

It was losing this childhood vision that made you a lower-grade achiever. The process of growing-up, and the subsequent learnt false perceptions of 'reality', may have made you set your sights lower than necessary. Successful, focused people are often very child-like in this one respect: they see dreams as reality and turn them into just that, leaving the rest of us marvelling at their courage. Like willful children they are also very inventive and focused on achieving their goals.

Children are natural 'Towards Thinkers', i.e. they see what they want and work out how to get it in the most simple way possible. This method of 'Towards Thinking' is going to be a fundamental part of your new philosophy of life.

Your personal potential is at least twenty times greater than you imagine, and so is your ability to get what you want. It's not knowing what you want in the first place that is going to cause major difficulties.

Growing up often means learning to become cynical about dreams and more comfortable with the barriers to achievement because they oppose action and effort, both of which cause apprehension. Children have little to lose in terms of possessions and self-maintained security and so will lock on to new wants. Adults are too busy holding on to their current acquisitions and comforts to let any drop as they reach for something better.

**Repeat after me:**
You will have been brought up on cynical sayings that made you wary of change, like:

> 'Out of the frying pan, into the fire.'
> 'Better the devil you know...'
> 'A bird in the hand is worth two in the bush.'
> 'Pride comes before a fall.'

Planning is essential to your success strategy, but gibbering caution isn't. Ask a small child what they want to be when they grow up and they will inevitably aim at the career jugular. Not just a sportsman/woman, but a medal winner. Not just a singer, but one with a number one single in the charts.

Fast forward a few years and what we consider 'real-life considerations' have often left their sad little snail-trails all over that free-thinking sense of ambition.

So maybe your potential needs a touch of freeing up? Perhaps you should have an injection of creativity into your life-plan? How much of what stands between you and whatever you consider to be personal success exists in reality and how much in your own mind?

How large a part do you feel your thinking and mental attitude play in your successes and failures?

Break that up into a percentage. Create a mental pie-chart, if that helps.

Take a few moments to consider this basic but vital question. Weigh up the factors that have contributed to past successes and failures, including the occasions where you gave up on an ambition, or didn't even try in the first place. Now move to your future and the goals you have brought with you as you started this book.

What percentage do you rate your attitude in its effect on those outcomes? Write down the answer.

We would rate it as high as 70% or over in most cases.

That's not to say that a positive mental attitude is all you need to be successful. Only an idiot would rate their chances based purely on enthusiasm and self-belief. Yet a lot of these idiots exist. The attitude is there. The confidence is in place. They believe they have a right to get what they want in life. The only things that are missing are the skills, talent and hard work. 'If I want something badly enough I can get it' is their motto. But what they mean is: 'I can get it on a plate.' Wanting is only part of the achievement plan. Which is why this book will examine every facet of that plan in a practical way.

## Dream on

Turning dreams into reality is very much part of this book's game plan but keeping some daydreams as merely daydreams is vital, too.

Three key messages:

1. Think big but think real.
2. Don't be too sparing with your perception of that reality.
3. Become an obsessive – don't be put off at the first obstacle, real or imagined.

When you try to think 'realistically' you will naturally tend to err on the side of caution. False, untested negativity takes over and you put a lid on your own potential.

These false perceptions will have started when you were a child.

Parents are inclined to urge caution as a survival reflex. They also tend to tell you that you can only 'do your best', leaving the back door open for you to accept failure. As a result you are unlikely to have ever tested your potential to anywhere near its limits. The chances are your risk assessment functions are flawed as well.

Stretch yourself and your horizons. One of the objectives of this book is to challenge your existing thinking and your perception of what is and isn't possible.

## Brain-power

The self-created, imagined barrier is going to be your greatest enemy on the path to success. Your biggest battles en route will be with yourself and your own mind. Your brain is your best friend, and your deadliest foe.

Challenge historical assumptions, especially those based on what you can and cannot achieve. Past failures are no guarantee of future ones. Only stop trying when you have to.

To separate the dreams you'll be converting into reality from those best stored as fantasies you need to start with a simple brainstorm.

## Creating your wish list

Turn to the blank work page in this book entitled dream work sheet (p.8), and fill it with anything you can think of that would come under the heading of 'What I would like to do or become.' There's no need to be sensible at this stage because you will be the only one reading the page. Don't discuss it or share it. Go with the flow and allow yourself to include anything, even things you judge to be silly. Be trivial and esoteric. Reality can keep off this sheet for now – we'll start to get structured at the next stage.

There is no rush in compiling this page. It is not just a fun exercise, it is a return to those big childhood goals, before false 'realities' set in. Go for it. Delete nothing. You're not into your personal strategy yet, you're just preparing your brain for lift-off. Take an hour, a day or even a week. Pick a time when you feel relaxed and stress free.

Perhaps you have been so busy focusing on other people's wants that you have forgotten a lot of your own. You may also have your own wants confused with what other people have told you you should want. Keep other people's wants well off your wish list. 'Want-but-can't-have's', however, should stay on until we've clarified the word 'can't'.

If you fill this page go on to another. Paper is cheap and – remember – this is your first step towards success.

A thought to keep in mind as you write: more people spend time in later life regretting what they *didn't* do than what they did. By creating your 'wish list' now you will be working to avoid this regret later on.

## The whole picture

As you compile your page you will find some 'wants' occur in your head as visual images. You see who or what you wish for in a mental picture. This visualisation is an important process that is closely linked to the success or failure of your objectives, which is why you'll hear more about it later.

For a goal to turn into reality it needs to stimulate the visual part of your brain. Seeing what you want is a crucial stage in achieving it.

Overleaf are two simple diagrams that will help you visualise the building blocks for success.

# The Building Blocks for Success

Highlighted below are some of

the considerations that will help you

achieve your objective/s.

Think about:

The foundation

The structure

The bond of each block

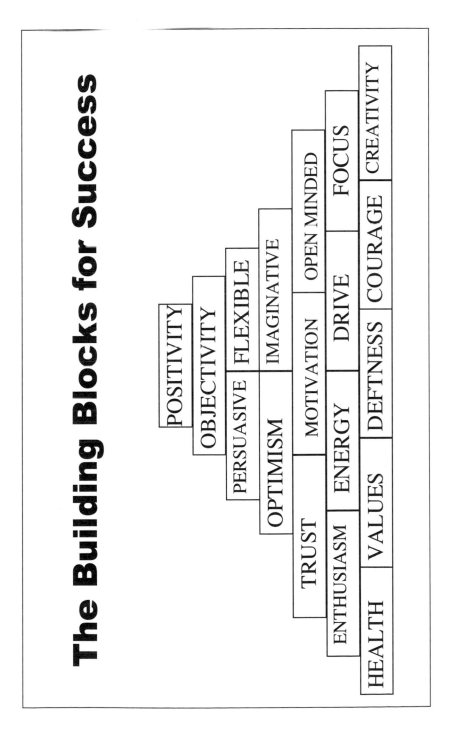

The Building Blocks for Success

**Work page 1**

## Dream Work Sheet

Back to the launch pad, though. When your dream work sheet is complete let it lie fallow for at least a week. Call time and then put it away, and don't look at it or think about it.

Then go back to it with an objective eye. Keep yourself tuned into the child's mentality, though. Don't turn into a disapproving adult. Somebody has to do or achieve these things, remember? And that somebody will be the only one who did not hear the voice of caution or disapproval. They will be impervious to the words 'can't' or 'shouldn't'. Your sole focus at this stage should be 'want to', which may or may not turn into a 'will'.

## The buzz

Look through your sheet, clutching a red marker pen in one hand, and underline the 'wants' that give you a physical buzz as you read them. Your body is going to be used in the same way a water-diviner uses a forked twig. Look out for any twitches of excitement or leaks of adrenalin associated with any of your ideas. Too illogical for you? Do you think your life plans require Vulcan-like decision-making?

Learn to cherish your deeper responses. Emotions are an intrinsic part of our survival programming. Smaller strategies can suffer from the intrusion of emotional response but you should learn to cherish the positive gut reaction when you work on bigger plans and decisions.

Gut reactions are precious, as they are your body's response to a good idea. Your brain will be slow to commit at this stage because you've been smothering it with messages of caution for years, but your stomach or your pulse-rate will know how to spot a potential winner.

Goals, ambitions and ideas that fail to excite you will rarely work because they will not be what you truly want. This is the first stirring of the passion that will keep you moving forward, even when the odds start stacking up against you. It is an infallible guide, even though it will need the intervention of logic and sense to maintain the practicalities. Never ignore it and never move into a strategy that doesn't include it. What fails to excite fails to sustain on the path towards success.

Now create your specific wish list on the following page, which is divided into two columns.

## Work page 2

**Wish List**

Take a red-pen wish from the dream work sheet and transfer it to the left-hand column of the wish list.

In the right-hand column – alongside it – write down the reality of the wish. Imagine you have achieved it already. What is the actual 'doing' of it like? What does it entail?

Forget the pinnacle of the achievement at the moment and work out what the day-to-day reality will be like.

For instance, you may wish to start up your own business. Of course you will have seen it being successful, but now is the time to imagine what that success actually feels like. What hours are you working? What is your level of commitment? How hard are you working?

Or perhaps you are off to live on a desert island. Start to imagine the reality of that life. How compatible is it with the things you truly enjoy?

Tony Blair must have wanted to be Prime Minister. Bill Clinton must have wanted to be President. Those achievements would be on a par to sailing round the world single-handedly. But how many of us would enjoy the reality of the job of state figurehead? What about the hours, the stresses and the loss of personal freedom? How many celebrities court fame and then complain about the lack of privacy it brings?

This is where you will begin to sort your goals from your dreams. Dreams are essential for happiness, but knowing they are just dreams will prevent you from feeling regret later in life about not trying to convert them into reality. This is vital for your future happiness and potential for contentment.

Keep goals and dreams in separate compartments. This avoids the: 'I always wanted to be a rock star but I had to pay the mortgage, and then the kids came along, and then it was too late because my hair was falling out...' stuff.

If it is a goal you will stick it on your strategy-planner and go for it. If not, you can dream away to your heart's content about getting up on stage and jamming with the Stones, but you should enjoy the fiction of the idea, rather than allow it to lead to resentment and discontent.

To see the difference between the dream and the goal note how many leading businessmen will use their planned goal to achieve what was probably a childhood dream. Or, in other words, they buy a football club! The whole thing then turns pear-shaped, they plummet in public popularity and their core business can suffer from neglect. Which was the dream and which the goal? Someone should have told them before it was too late.

## How happiness creates misery

It is true that you can't buy happiness. However, that is no reason for staying poor. Status is another thing that does not come with a written guarantee of well-being and contentment.

Perhaps all bosses and millionaires spend their time wearing a suitably dour expression in public and then grinning like Cheshire cats as they quaff champagne in the privacy of their own homes? The truth is that a lot of rich and powerful people look miserable because they *are* miserable; completely brassed off because they attained the wealth or position they had been striving for, but discovered it did little to change their mood or state of mind.

Money and power can only increase pleasure if they bring you what you want.

Lack of either can cause misery, but neither money nor status are capable of instilling true happiness by themselves, it is their by-products that can stimulate the pleasure.

Wealth is personal and it is associated with need. You don't have to be rich to feel wealthy.

Close your eyes and think back to a time in your life when you were truly happy. Spend a moment re-living that occasion. What were you doing? Gazing at a cheque? Counting piles of coins? Running your fingers through the notes in your wallet? Relishing the fact that you could hire or fire and tell other people what to do? Probably not.

Your images of past happiness are probably relationship or experience-related. The things you enjoy most are possibly made all the more precious by the rarity of the experience. You may have imagined a one-off treat. Or it could be the uniqueness of the experience that made it precious: a special holiday; eating a wonderful meal; getting married, etc. Most of these experiences would be devalued if they happened too frequently. Humans quickly learn to take even the most impressive events or experiences for granted. Then we get bored and start looking around for more.

## Exceeding expectations

Exceeding expectations is a formula for happiness. If you get more than you are expecting out of a day or experience then you will be happy. If your expectations are met then you will be neither happy nor unhappy. If the situation or experience fails to live up to your expectations then you will be unhappy.

'Having it all' usually brings an increased level of expectation. Sometimes those expectations become too high to exceed and then the formula for happiness no longer applies.

Buying your first car was probably an exciting, pleasing experience. You may have saved for it and obtained an inflated degree of pride at the ownership, even if it was an old banger. As you get older and purchase more cars the pleasure may decrease, unless the quality of each car purchased increases dramatically. If you are on to your third Porsche or Bentley you may be disappointed to discover the 'buzz' of purchase has lessened and even become negligible.

This is not to say that you should shed tears for the extremely wealthy, but that you shouldn't make the assumption that material goods, power and status will lead to happiness. People who start out with a miserable personality usually stay that way despite the odd lottery win.

So what is the price of your own personal happiness? What do you need for success and how can you ensure you monitor that success effectively? Can you stray down the path of others' values by mistake? What is the formula for targeting your own level of desired attainment and how can you keep your focus in the face of outside pressures and expectations?

For the answers to all this and more, read on...

**Review and work plan**

1. Make a distinction between your dreams and your goals.
2. Think big. But also cherish the smaller goals.
3. Be realistic in your goals – but stretch your perception of what is 'realistic' to the limits.
4. Create a 'want' list  – brainstorm goals and objectives. Revisit it after a week and underline the ones that create a gut reaction when you read them.
5. Put the 'wants' on a sheet of paper with the 'doing' list beside each one.
6. Begin to feel the reality of your dreams.

# CHAPTER **2**

---

# *Sieze the day*

'I grew up with two brothers. As in many families they ridiculed me for being female, for not being able to run as fast and so on. My inner drive probably stems from a determination to prove that I was as good – if not better – than them... Once the business started I found it rewarded me with so much pleasure that my enthusiasm no longer needed any impetus. I simply enjoy what I do.'

**Stephanie Manuel, founder of Stagecoach teaching business, quoted in *Success Now* magazine**

Do you like pep-talks? If not, skip this chapter.

First some key facts:

1. The British have the longest working hours in Europe.
2. Tea and lunch breaks are becoming extinct in the workplace – often voluntarily.
3. An increasing amount of staff are 'having' to take work home with them in the evenings.
4. The cult of 'down-sizing' or 'business re-engineering' means less staff doing more work.

Or, to put it in plain English, you may well be one of those who are working too hard.

This may have several negative effects on your ability to plan and realise your personal goals:

1. You are too busy to think.
2. You are too tired to 'do'.
3. You are so caught up with 'fire-fighting', i.e. dealing with life's smaller emergencies as they break out, that you have lost track of your long-term goals.
4. Your brain is suffering from 'premature corporate burn-out'. You're using the cells up too quickly on the wrong things.
5. Your perceptions are distorted. Your life lacks balance.

## Hamster wheels

A question: have you ever suffered a brief pang of empathy while watching a hamster running its legs off on its exercise wheel? Do those bulging eyes and frantic little legs putting all that effort into no apparent achievement look in any way familiar? Do you identify with the little creature's plight?

Work – and even life – can feel just like that hamster wheel. And, no, that's not the most profound statement ever made. But it is true, all the same.

## The ancient mariner

The point of this chapter is for you to get your life into some sort of context before it's too late.

By too late we mean you need to avoid becoming one of those bitter people who suddenly become aware that they're too old to get anywhere and so resort to bending the ear of anyone close by, like The Ancient Mariner, telling the sad tale of what might have been if only...

The blame never lies with them. Life stacked the pack against them and they were dealt all the bad cards. If only they'd married someone else... not had a mortgage to pay... taken up that job offer... moved to that other place... etc, etc. They could have been a contender. They could have hit the big time. Only something stopped them. Probably themselves, only that truth is too hard to face. So they carry on blaming others.

*Judi writes:* 'I have my own Ancient Mariner tale. When I was young I wanted to be a ballet star. I was a good dancer but I got chucked out of ballet school, aged nine. Life had defeated me, I had grown too tall. There was no way I would achieve my ambition, so I gave up.

'When I went to my first grown-up ballet, many years later, guess who pranced out on stage? A tall ballerina. So how did she get there? Simple: either nobody told her she couldn't dance or, if they did, she didn't listen. She didn't hear the "no". The same is true of many successful people.'

So... how to avoid Ancient Mariner syndrome?

Now is the time to take an objective view of your own life. Difficult? Of course it is. You're right there in the middle of it, doing your best and muddling through each day, nose to the grindstone. Your life is an experience you are totally connected to, so how can you pull away and review? One leading recruitment consultant told us that organisations are currently keeping staff too busy to job-hunt. They see the ad, tell themselves they're going to apply for the job, intend getting their CV up to date, but then two weeks later they pick up the same paper and find the ad is gone and they've missed the boat.

One way to manage and prioritise your time is to make a log.

People make logs for many different reasons but mainly to do with time. Time is a precious commodity and later on in this book we will be showing you how to log it to create space for your success plan.

This first log, though, will be based on feelings and associated emotions.

**Work page 3**

### Emotions Log

For this emotions log your page will be divided into time segments but only to calculate feelings and achievements. Start it on a week that has all the appearance of being as near to average as possible.

Each day should be divided into half-hour segments. Use four coloured pens and just draw a line to signify time spent on different activities (different lengths representing different times), using one pen to denote happiness, one for mild pleasure, one for discontent or boredom and one for unhappiness or misery. Under each coloured horizontal line write how that stretch of time was occupied.

Those of you who aren't inspired by coloured lines might prefer to draw a graph of each day, charting the emotional highs and lows.

Be honest about your emotions log and show it to no-one, for obvious reasons. Never chart what you suppose should be a high just because you imagine you ought to have felt good at that moment. If sitting watching an episode of a soap on TV rates highly then so be it. This is a psychological experiment so there is no need for guilt trips at this moment.

How much time do you allow each week for the pursuit or development of happiness? And how many of your happinesses were 'Towards', rather than 'Away From'?

## Towards and away from pleasures

There are two different ways of reaching pleasure or happiness, the 'Towards' or the 'Away From' routes. An 'Away From' high will have appeared on your log if you rated the moment you get into your car and drive away from work as a high spot. Your happiness has come as a result of leaving something that was making you unhappy.

'Towards' highs occur if you actively engage in something that gives you pleasure. Getting drunk can be either 'Towards' or 'Away From', depending on whether you drink to get jolly or drink to forget.

Once you have logged the ratio of high and low spots in your week, divide the highs into 'Towards' or 'Away From' motivators.

How many of them occurred as a result of pure, looked for pleasure and how many as a result of the pain going away? 'Towards' pleasures are often less easy to achieve than the 'Away From' ones, but the results have to be more rewarding. Allocate time and energy to build more 'Towards' pleasures into your life.

And what about your overall goals? How about those visions of success that this book is going to coach you towards achieving? Are those goals 'Towards' or 'Away From'? Are you inspired by a vision of how things could be or motivated away from how they are at present?

'Away From' motivators are part of the landscape of achievement. You may have a burning desire to 'prove something' to old mates, teachers or relatives who think you are worthless; you may have recently divorced and want to break out of feelings of low self-esteem. Maybe you want to out-do a sibling, friend or colleague who is a high achiever and evokes feelings of competition or jealousy? Do you just want a better car or house than the one your neighbour's just bought? Perhaps you just want to prove something to yourself.

These emotions will spur you on. However – and you knew this was brewing up into a 'however', didn't you? – you should also take a long look at the forward view. Visions need to be positive. They should fill your horizon. Your motivation should be towards that vision, not purely away from your current view.

Study the purity of your objectives. What do you want to see most, the achievement itself within touching distance, or the looks on other people's faces when you tell them you've reached it?

Goals should be set for the value of their pleasure to *you*, not to inspire envy in other people. Your path towards your goal may be long and difficult. What will you do if those other folk fade out of your life before you get there? Parents have been known to pass on before their offspring 'make something of themselves'. Will you be just as happy standing ranting at the family plot?

Always understand your main motivational factor for any attempted goal. Know what inspires and drives you. Evaluate that emotion and dissect it. Is it sustainable? Is it tangible? Is it achievable? Your emotional state will be crucial to your goal development and achievement.

Primary emotions were once vital to our survival, affecting our feelings, our bodily response and our behavioural response to stimulus.

Primary emotions are:
  Fear
  Disgust
  Sadness
  Surprise
  Anticipation
  Anger
  Acceptance
  Joy.

Fear, for instance, would be induced by life-threatening situations and evoke a physical response – sweating, shallow breathing, increased heart rate, etc – as well as a behavioural response – fight or flight.

Any of these emotions could be involved as motivators towards your own personal goals. All of them can produce a strong response and behavioural reaction if they are induced during your goal-journey.

Secondary emotions are those that are triggered by your own thoughts or imagination. Secondary emotions are usually the result of two or more primary emotions combining. They include:

  Aggression
  Contempt
  Optimism
  Love
  Remorse
  Disappointment
  Submission
  Awe.

Understanding the primitive function of emotions can help you evaluate their value to your plans.

Anger, for instance, has been known to stimulate success. Someone who has been told they are a loser may use stimulated anger and turn it into the energy needed to fuel success. In the right circumstances anger will produce fight and persistence. It can also be destructive, though.

Fear can be harnessed to aid your goal-plan. It's important you understand the risks involved and plan ways of eliminating or decreasing them. The primitive fear response, though, was to run away. Uncontrolled fear may lead to you avoiding your goals altogether.

Fear of failure can be a very destructive emotion. Like a phobia it is nurtured through avoidance. You may have failed in a similar venture to the one you are considering. Sometimes the similarity of the situations can be small enough to be laughable. You may dread making a business presentation because you fluffed your lines in the school nativity play. Your emotions surrounding that ancient event could be strong enough to haunt you, making you avoid any situation that is remotely similar. Or perhaps you have failed to apply for a job or promotion interview because you lacked confidence in your ability to do the job if you got it.

So is it better to embark on your goal-plan emotion-free? Is pure unadulterated logic the safest approach?

Emotions can be destructive if left unchecked. Irrational decisions can scupper the soundest business plan. However, creativity and gut-reaction may be vital ingredients to your success. If your goals are challenging ones you will need determination, courage and desire to see you through. Lack of emotion leads to indifference.

The left side of the brain is the analytical side, while the right is responsible for creative, intuitive thought. Use the left side to spearhead your plans, creating and plotting objectives and goals, while the right side and your heart provide the passion to drive you on.

Optimism is rarely a logical emotion and yet you will need plenty of it – plus the positive thought patterns it encourages – if you are going to achieve your life-long goals.

Chart your emotions just as you chart your success plan. Analysing feelings can be difficult at first, but writing them down is important. How do you feel when you think about your targeted goal/s? What emotions do they evoke? How do you feel when you begin to consider the changes and steps you will have to take to achieve those goals? It is vital you start to consider your emotions now as they play an important role in your mental preparation stages.

List your emotions under three headings:

1. Lifelong baggage.
2. Sustaining the present.
3. Future changes.

## 1. Lifelong baggage

This needs careful analysing if it is not going to cause problems. When the conscious brain records an event and stores it away in the subconscious it will often pack it up with an accompanying emotion. This is useful for survival in the wild but the system becomes flawed when the perception causes a faulty emotional memory for future reference.

### Goal-phobia

These flaws will often show up in the case of phobias. An irrational fear of a thing or situation can be induced by a single bad memory. A child who gets locked in the toy cupboard may feel fear. The fear is largely irrational – there was no harm done and the situation may not have lasted for more than a few minutes – but panic was produced and may be reproduced again each time that individual is placed in a closed or crowded environment. The panic has become the triggered response.

When the brain matures the conscious mind is unable to override the initial command of fear and panic, even when the adult knows there is nothing threatening in the situation. It is as though the senses take control of the brain and claustrophobia becomes the order of the day.

The same will be true of a fear of spiders. You know that spiders aren't life-threatening in this country, but your emotional and physical response may be one of pure fear. When the conscious and the subconscious brain are in conflict the subconscious will usually win.

Your lifelong baggage can scupper success in the same way. Old negative associations bring about flawed emotional responses and you may forget to question them. Tackle old fears and worries that may be threatening your positivity by analysing them objectively.

'Spider' fears are the ones you deem to be irrational. Perhaps you are worried about looking stupid if your scheme fails. Maybe you hear the voice of a teacher or parent telling you you stand no chance of success because you are stupid or lazy. These bits of baggage need throwing out.

'Tiger' baggage is the genuine survival stuff. No-one would argue that a fear of tigers was irrational. Feeling uneasy about a situation due to stored memory of something similar may indeed be helpful. Rational caution may be necessary to avoid you falling headlong into failure. A pilot will value lessons learnt through past experience and know how to deal with threatening situations in future.

Very few goals come risk-free but past experience can either help or hinder you in your risk-assessment and subsequent planning, depending on the rationality of your learned emotional response.

## 2. Sustaining the present

Positive emotions will sustain you as you work your way to success. The steps toward that success can be uncomfortable or hard and it will be the sense of excitement, anticipation, resolve, determination, anger or whatever that will help to drive you on. You may be playing totally against the odds with your goal-plan and need the passion and the vision to sustain you in the face of conflicting advice.

## 3. Future changes

Understand that it is possible that your goal, and the journey towards achieving it, may change your current emotional responses. Also, that achieving that goal may not induce the expected emotional feedback.

You are capable of emotional evolution. Changing circumstances can cause a change in response. You may learn patience, tolerance, anger, stoicism, calm etc, etc.

You may like to think about developing certain emotional qualities that will be necessary for your personal achievement. Look into the future right now and write a list of emotional qualities you feel would help you achieve your goals.

**Work page 4**

**Emotional Qualities**

## A personal touch

Make your vision of success your own, or the pleasure of success might be tainted by others' under-reaction. Do things because *you* want to, not to make others' jealous. There is no need to be selfish, though. If your goals can be shared then the pleasure may be doubled.

## Seeing the future

If you have difficulty charting your vision of success try visualisation, a technique we will spend more time on later in this book.

Look forward. Tell yourself that you are now a successful person, that you have achieved many things in your life and are happy. Repeat this idea several times until it begins to stimulate your subconscious and creativity. Once you can feel your imagination beginning to kick in close your eyes and focus on nothing. Repeat the idea of success achievement. Keep telling yourself that you have arrived at the level of happiness that you had as your goal. Now begin to let the pictures paint the reality. See yourself being successful. See yourself being happy. Don't rush the sequence. Allow the image to emerge from your subconscious, not conscious, mind. The conscious will be tainted by outside expectations but your subconscious should supply the proper picture.

## Mental imaging

What did you see when you focused on that successful self? An image of yourself climbing out of a stretch limo? Or singing on stage before a packed and adoring audience? Were you walking through corridors of offices in a company you owned? Or were you out in the countryside gazing at a beautiful view?

You may have imagined any or none of these things. What you have to do, though, is to get in touch with your own vision of pleasure, success and happiness. That vision must belong to you and be unadulterated by others' perceptions or expectations. Otherwise success and achievement will never come to mean the same as happiness, pleasure and contentment for you.

## Clichés

Clichés always receive a bad press, though some can be useful. If you work in a spiral of stress and panic over unrealistic deadlines, fire-fighting like crazy; if you worry about business matters and take those worries home with you to the extent that you are ruining your own time; if your life lacks planning, or an overall purpose, then throwing a few well-chosen clichés into the picture can only help, for instance:

'This is my one and only life, it's not a dress rehearsal.'
Or: 'Treat each day as though it were your last' (difficult), and the best of the lot, 'Seize the day.'

When you plan your life on a daily or yearly basis always be aware of your mortality. You need to take a look at the big picture, understanding that one day it will all end. This knowledge should not be depressing, but it should affect your decisions. In your imagination you should start at the end and then look back. How will your life look to you in retrospect? What could be your greatest regrets? And what will you perceive as your greatest achievements? What advice do you think the future you would give the current you right now? When in doubt, go for it.

Do you feel that the overall vision of your life escapes you because you are too bogged down in the day-to-day details? Do life events just happen to you or do you plan them and set them as goals? Do you control your own future or does the urgency of the present control you and scupper your potential?

The present is the only reality. Handle the 'now' and you begin to take control of your future. Plan to control that future now but start now, too. Prevarication is pointless. Watch joggers or cyclists. Once they have begun their journey they make every attempt not to stop on the way. The jogger will jog on the spot while waiting for traffic and the cyclist will make every effort not to put his or her feet on the ground when waiting for the lights. Why? Because it is more difficult to get going again once you stop and the momentum grinds to a halt. Start now and keep going, even if you jog on the spot for a while.

Navel-gazing is vital at this stage of your planning. This is the point at which you take a step back out of your life to see

whether it is on course or not. How do you feel right now?
Tick one of the following:

Happy? ☐
Contented? ☐
Dissatisfied? ☐
Unfulfilled? ☐
Overworked? ☐
Bored? ☐
Depressed? ☐
Stimulated? ☐
Inspired? ☐
Motivated? ☐
Creative? ☐
Energetic? ☐
Mentally exhausted? ☐

Negative emotions or experiences can be useful only if they
are part of an overall plan. Doctors go through a period of
training and working long hours that may seem unbearable, but
which are seen as a means to an end. An actor going on months
of soul-destroying castings and working in a cafe to make ends
meet will get through this low point because they have their eyes
fixed on the stars. People who start up their own businesses go
through long periods of overwork while they get the business
off the ground. Buying a new home may mean a crippling
mortgage but you will know that your income will go up and
the burden will ease.

The point is that all this negativity is used as a means to an
end. It's when there is no end or goal in sight that this sort of
life can be stressful or unbearable. Nobody in their right mind
would chose to risk life and limb just for something to do. It is
the thought of getting the chequered flag that spurs the racing
driver on.

You need to be clear of your own goal before you embark
on your journey. If the objective is sound you may find the
hardships en route bearable. If you are unfocused in your vision
then the smallest set-back will seem insurmountable and quitting
might seem the best option.

## Shooting yourself in the foot

Let's get back to the Tall Poppy syndrome. Imagine yourself three-quarters of the way up a mountain. Imagine looking up at the peak and yelling out: 'Oh no, that's not really what I want after all!' If you plan your goals without using a fair amount of imagination that's exactly what could happen to you in your quest for success.

Some reasons why that goal may not look so good once you get close up to it:

1. As we have said, it's what someone else wanted for you, not what you wanted.
2. You are frightened by it.
3. You suddenly realise the commitment involved in that particular success.
4. You suddenly see how other people's expectations of you became raised the more successful you became. Your own success was a hard act to follow.
5. You become frightened that success was a one-off, that you just got lucky, while others are expecting more.
6. You suddenly see that success involved a lot of hard work.
7. Your own success makes you feel guilty.
8. Your success makes others envious, which means you lose friends and/or family and get lonely.
9. You gain new friends but doubt their sincerity. How many of them are only there because of your success?
10. Once you get to the top the only way is down. Be kind to others as you climb because you never know when you're going to need them on the descent.

Now these are demons you are going to have to deal with. Maybe we shouldn't have said anything, just sat back and let you find out for yourself when you got there, but you wouldn't have liked us very much at that point, would you?

We want you to be *happy* and successful, not just successful. Which is why we're warning you about the potential down-side before you get there. Or before you get within sniffing distance and then self-destruct when the reality of it all hits you. Before you become another tall poppy that lops off its own head.

Be the tall poppy that keeps its head. Allow yourself to grow.

## Review and work plan

1. Create an emotions log to discover the highs and lows in your daily life.
2. Differentiate between the 'Towards' and 'Away From' pleasures.
3. Start to study your success goals. Are they motivated by 'Towards' or 'Away From' thinking?
4. Analyse the quality of the motivational factors surrounding each of your objectives. Write down the feelings attached to each goal.
5. List emotions under three headings:

   a) Lifelong baggage.
   b) Sustaining the present.
   c) Future changes.

   Which will help you achieve your goals and which will hinder?
6. Start to visualise your personal success.

# CHAPTER 3

# Packing for the journey

> 'Dealing with success is quite difficult. You're meant to enjoy the whole process. It's a bit like being pregnant is for a woman. It's meant to be all rosy and you're not meant to complain, so you keep it all inside, which can be hard.'
>
> **Ewan MacGregor**
>
> 'The need to survive gave me the confidence to know I was good at the job.'
>
> **Lynn Brooks, Brooks Estate Agents**

Before you set off en route to success let's have a glance at the packing list, as the success of your journey may depend on what you chose to carry along with you, as well as what you decide to leave behind.

## Scuppering your own success

There are several factors that will be critical to your success. You know each and every one of them, but that is no reason for not dealing with them here because once you are all fired up with the enthusiasm of your plan you may be oblivious to the obvious until it's too late.

Negativity arises when you worry about a plan or journey to the point where you never embark on it or do so without enjoyment. What we are going to do in this chapter is not negative, though. By studying your potential barriers you can plan how to attack them. Most of them can be thrown out of your luggage straight away. It's just that sometimes they sneak in there when your back is turned.

## Your six greatest hurdles to success

So what are these qualities that can create havoc with your success?

## 1. Stupidity

Just for a kick-off. Not a lack of intellectual thought, because heaven knows there are enough successful people out there who flunked at school, but that basic sort of cleverness. The stuff that makes you a visionary with good sense, someone who understands the value of planning and hard work and who knows when they are behaving like an idiot or when they're doing well.

Stupid doesn't mean making mistakes, it means making mistakes and learning nothing from the experience! Stupid means thinking you can have it all just by wanting and expecting. Stupid means thinking success and happiness are somehow a right and not a privilege. Successful people are capable of doing stupid things but stupid people are rarely, if ever, capable of being successful.

## 2. Negativity

One thing you're going to have to jettison on that path to success is your Negative Inner Voice, and it's going to hurt. This voice has been with you for so much of your life it feels like a pal and that's just how it acts, whispering into your subconscious all those wonderful reasons for not trying your best.

Worried about failure? Your Negative Inner Voice will supply you with 1001 reasons to quit before you start. Nervous or fearful about a situation? Your Negative Inner Voice will fuel your fears, presenting the worst case in any given situation.

## Survival

There is a point to the voice, unfortunately, which is what makes it so hard to ignore. In the past it was the voice of survival, warning you about true danger and stimulating your survival system. Unfortunately, it is in perilous situations that we often choose to ignore it, driving too quickly in the car or taking too many risks with our health or well-being. When that voice should be there to warn you – maybe when you light up a cigarette or reach for that last glass of wine before driving home – you'll often find it's playing dumb. Take it to a business presentation or job interview, though, and suddenly it starts to sing for its supper. Some classic quotes from the Negative Inner Voice:

> 'Mondays are always the worst day of the week.'
> 'I just know they'll ask me the most difficult questions.'
> 'That client always causes me problems.'
> 'I know they won't like me.'
> 'There's no point pitching for that business, I won't get it.'
> 'I expect that job will have gone before I get there.'
> 'That restaurant's always fully booked on Saturday, there's no point trying for a table.'
> 'Why do I always get in the longest queue?'
> 'There's no point trying to change, it won't do any good.'
> 'I'm never lucky.'
> 'I can see they don't like me.'

In terms of self-help and stimulation, this Negative Inner Voice is about the worst you can do. It swivels your focus around onto the 'can't'.

## You get exactly what you expect

Oh, and by the way, it is a self-fulfilling prophesy. Think in that way and what you hear is usually about what you get. You allow it to attract you to disaster like metal to a magnet. It has a good track-record of being right because it creates its own failure.

Think you'll do badly and you probably will. Expect the worst and you won't be disappointed. Flirt with failure in that way and the first set-back will seem like a sign from the gods, warning you to give up and go home.

Positive self-belief helps overcome most mental hurdles.

Negative self-belief will leave you fallen at the first fence and unable to get back up onto your feet again.

So how to get rid of this voice of doom and gloom?

1. Recognise it for the ignorant, troublesome, tiresome little tyke that it is.
2. Identify it the minute it starts to open its mouth.
3. Tell it to shut up and clear off. Get angry.

But don't turn your back for one minute or it will be crawling back into your luggage and you'll be lugging it along en route.

Use work page 5 opposite to compile quotes, sayings and one-off words from your Negative Inner Voice. Write them down as they come out. Then read them back and see how they sound. You may laugh or you may cry when you realise how dumb the voice is. If it was a friend you'd have jettisoned them years ago.

The Negative Inner Voice is the voice of doom, gloom, pessimism and paranoia. It thrives on the fact that it is rarely challenged. Why? Because we haven't got the guts, that's why.

'Expect the worst and you can't be hurt' is the catch phrase of the pessimist.

'I always tell myself the worst things will happen and that everything that can go wrong will go wrong' one businesswoman told us, 'Then when it does I'm not too upset because I was expecting it. If it doesn't I'm pleased.'

## Embracing failure

Courting failure is a seriously flawed technique. How can failure hurt less if you know you didn't really try in the first place because you were expecting to fail anyway?

Silencing the Negative Inner Voice leads to a technique known as becoming an Inverse Paranoid. Instead of expecting the worst, expect the best. Expect the worst and that's pretty much what you get, so perhaps the opposite is also true!

**Work page 5**

**Famous Quotes and One-Liners, courteousy of my Negative Inner Voice**

## 3. Laziness

We're all prone to laziness! Take any average workaholic and there's a lazy person inside, waiting to get out. That's why workaholics behave as they do. They're frightened to stop in case they can't start up again. Once that settee or beach recliner get a grip you may find yourself unable to get up. Take a breather and it may be for life.

Are you a lazy person? Do you love doing nothing? Is Homer Simpson your role-model? Yes? Then maybe you should make 'doing very little' be your objective. I'm not joking – at least you'll feel happy and will have achieved what you wanted. Why work your socks off all day otherwise, unless you're planning on the sort of long-term laziness that requires a pool, servants and an expensive yacht to achieve?

If doing nothing makes you happy then there is little point creating an objective that requires a lot of hard work. Unless you're expecting to undergo a chameleon-like change, that is, which is unlikely. Starting your own business should be off the menu, for instance, unless you already have a massive amount of money and can employ others to run it from day one.

A lot of lazy people make the mistake of starting up their own business and then wondering why either:

a)   it goes bankrupt straightaway, or
b)   they're not happy.

It went bust because they lost interest and didn't put in the required amount of effort these things take, or they're not happy because they put in the work and it's killing them. Simple, isn't it? And foreseeable.

The lazy way to get rich is to buy a lottery ticket. If you can manage the walk to the shops, that is.

## 4. Can't be bothered

Ditto. Can you be bothered to succeed? Is the prize a big enough incentive or reward? Is the effort you're expecting worth it? Think long and hard about this one. Are you bothered enough about your objective? If not, you may well need to take a

corporate decision to give up before you start. Working hard for
something you don't really want, except in a 'Well, I suppose it
might be nice' kind of a way, is rarely a rewarding experience. If
you can't be bothered then the solution is easy: move out of the
way and make space for those who can.

Enjoy your lack of commitment, it's not a crime, but see it
as your choice, too. No-one has the right to force you to put
more effort into your life. Not everybody is made happy by effort.
Most animals are only driven by short-term needs to eat, have
sex, keep warm and acquire shelter. When all those needs are sated
they play around or fall asleep, and many humans are like that,
too. And why not?

One little favour if you fit that particular bill, though. When
you meet someone who has achieved a hard-won success don't
tell them that they're lucky. Pick your own path in life but don't
demean others en route. Luck rarely has anything to do with
success. Quite simply they put in the work while you didn't.

## 5. Blame baggage

If you don't achieve your goal who are you going to blame?
Have you already drawn up a list? Blame is too heavy and
unwieldy an emotion to take along on this trip.

Blame goes hand-in-hand with the word 'can't'. As long as you
can blame other people or circumstances for your own failures the
implication is that is just wasn't your fault. Neat, isn't it? Blame can
go back donkey's years. There are top professionals in business
blaming the failure of a promotion or sales presentation on
something that went wrong in their childhood. Blame is great
because you can toss it around everywhere and – unlike a
boomerang – it rarely comes back unless you decide to accept it.

### Blame-listing

Write your blame list now (overleaf) and get it over and done
with, or you'll be using it as an excuse for your own prophesied
failure. Whose fault will it be if you fail to reach you personal
objectives? Get the Hall of Blame Fame sorted out right away.

**Work page 6**

## Personal Blame List

Get the boot in now. Who has appeared on your list? Your mother? Brother? Teacher? A boss who is holding you back? A colleague who pinches your ideas? Your bank manager for not funding your fantasies? How big is your list?

Or is there only one name on it – your own?

Even leaders have a way of taking blame that makes it obvious they don't think the mess was their fault. Phrases like: 'As manager I have to accept that it is my job to take the blame for that mistake' or, in other words, 'Some-one in the team screwed up but I am big enough to shield them.'

Lack of self-blame implies lack of choice and control. If your failure is always down to someone else then what chance do you have of success?

Be big and accept the fact that you control your own destiny. Bad things may have happened in the past but the good thing about the past is that it no longer exists. You can pillage it for your own uses but what you don't want from your past is a load of excuses that ruin your present.

## It's my own fault if I fail

Sounds scary, doesn't it? Sort of windswept and lonely. However, it is also a freeing, empowering statement. Still not happy with it? Try this then, because the two statements come hand-in-hand:

IF I SUCCEED IT IS DOWN TO ME. I CREATE MY OWN SUCCESS.

Sound more positive? This way there will only be one back to pat when you get there. Ever watch the Oscars? Remember the bit where the winners thank an endless list of people and pets for putting them up there on stage? Did you look at their faces as they spoke, though? They know who they really want to thank for their success. They know it was down to themselves and themselves alone. *Their* talent and good looks. If the rest of the team were so hot they'd be up there on their own merit.

Delegate, get help and advice but know that ultimately – save for war, pestilence and acts of God – the power to your own success or failure lies in your hands.

## 6. Making mistakes

Everyone makes mistakes in their life. Only some tend to carry those mistakes around with them for a bit longer than others. Again, there is no room in the luggage for old scars. Learn from errors if there is anything to be learnt and then try the following technique: CANCEL AND CONTINUE.

Let the memory drop. Don't be scarred. Watch those ice-skaters when they're in competition. When they fall they go flying on the ice but in less than a second they're up again and carrying on with their routine as though nothing had happened. Why? Well what is to be gained in trying to go forward while you're looking backward? If the brain fixates on the fall it makes another tumble more likely. Success requires confidence. Falls create future unsteadiness unless the focus is re-negotiated back to your objectives.

Success is often seen as a solo journey and is therefore judged to be selfish. You are doing what *you* want, achieving what *you* want to achieve. The time and effort involved can be extraordinary. The guilt that can result from this can be devastating to the unsuspecting and unwary.

Where else could that time and effort be employed? Who may you feel is missing out because you're busy on your wish-fulfilment trail? Is the balance going to be right? Can you feed the goldfish, phone your mother, wind the baby, bake bread, weed the garden, nurture friends and build your own empire all at the same time? Did Buzz Aldrin miss anyone's birthday while he was walking on the moon? Does Bill Gates wash his own car?

Guilt is a very invasive emotion. It is also very personal. One person's guilt trip is another's snort of ridicule or disbelief. You may feel guilty at the sight of your partner and kids downing yet another TV dinner because you were too busy with your own career path to cook something yourself. Or maybe you're the confident type who can put your mother on hold on the phone while you take a call from your stockbroker on the other line.

One leading businesswoman can guarantee a roomful of tearful executives every time she relates how her young daughter asked 'Are you my mummy?' while she read her a rare bedtime story. It's like a scythe to the legs of high-achievers and an almost comical mood-turner at conferences. From Wow! to Wah! in four easy words.

Guilt is a non-negotiable emotion because it is intrinsic, causing you grief before you know it. Perhaps the whole concept of being successful will cause you to feel guilty, not because the car needs a wax and the dog's started to learn how to use a can opener, but because you feel you don't deserve that wealth/power/comfortable lifestyle.

You are patently going to have to make decisions on this one. What are you prepared to sacrifice/juggle/put before success? What risks and gambles will you take with your existing happiness? More will be made of this point later. Just take a quick glance at the concept of guilt now, before it sneaks up and grabs you when you are not looking.

---

### Review and work plan
1. Start your packing list.
2. Jettison the negatives from the luggage.
3. Compile quotes from your Negative Inner Voice to become more objective about it.
4. Take responsibility and ownership:

   'It is my fault if I fail.'
   'My success is up to me.'
   'I create my own success.'

# CHAPTER 4

# *Feeling motivators*

> **On success**
>
> 'Success is about thinking big and thinking strategic. It's about building emotional relationships with people at work. Your work needs to become your hobby and you need focus and drive. It's looking beyond a salary. It's a love affair with work that transmits to other people.'
>
> **David Mitchell – Chief Executive of The Aston Group**

Now that you've jettisoned some of your negative baggage you need to decide what stuff's coming along in the hand luggage. What states of mind will help you achieve your goals? With the restraining mental attitudes dealt with where should your focus be turning to now?

As you have already seen in the previous chapter, emotional motivators need to be examined as they may help or hinder your goal-plan. Using the Towards/Away From concept, list your emotional motivators, e.g.

*Away From:*
    Frustration
    Boredom
    Guilt at wasting my life

Desire to get a life
Dysfunctional relationships at home
Lack of fulfilment, etc.

*Towards*:
Happiness
Excitement
Passion
Self-pride
Determination
Love
Revenge, etc.

Study the two lists once you have finished them. Especially the Towards list. These are the emotions you will be striving to work towards. They will be the rewards for your achievements. But how many of them will come with a guarantee? Are any unrealistic in terms of your ambitions?

Negative emotional rewards can be every bit as motivating as positive ones, and sometimes easier to achieve. Take the word *revenge*. How many sports people win in competition because they wish to take revenge on an opponent? Perhaps someone has humiliated them in competition in the past or maybe they have criticised them in the press prior to competition. How many international events are hyped into one country getting revenge on another for some non-sport related historical incident?

Revenge can inspire will to win and even give you that 'killer' edge, but – standing alone – it rarely sustains success in business in the same way it can on the sports field. Companies compete, but the competition will more often destroy and/or weaken both sides. Phyrric victories are usually the result of hostility-based success paths. Revenge-based elation can be a short-lived emotion and you may find you've been eased into a goal that was not of your own choosing because of it.

If you need the buzz of negative emotional satisfiers like revenge always check you have your path shored up with accompanying positives. Achieving your final goal should feed a greater desire than blood-lust. There needs to be something there to carry you further. Your rewards need to be positive as well as negative or you could end up the long-term loser.

## Fit for success

Short-term, 'easy' goals will probably be achievable without too much effort. But how about the training and preparation for the long-term, bigger stuff? Emotional fitness is vital, but you need to be physically and mentally prepared as well. Will-power and a strong mental attitude are more important to your success than your physical fitness, but being healthy certainly won't hurt.

## Brain-train

So what is mental fitness all about? Are there exercises you can do that will prepare your brain just as you would prepare your body by working out in a gym?

The first thing you need to understand is that your brain capacity is vast. Medical experts disagree on exactly how limitless your mental powers are, but the generally agreed fact is that you are capable of much more than you imagine.

To simplify: your brain functions in two ways – consciously and subconsciously. The conscious part of the brain takes in new information, makes decisions, learns new facts. Most of this is then stored away in the subconscious, often with associated emotional responses.

The subconscious is huge and it is largely non-judgmental. Imagine it to be a massive filing cabinet or storage space. The odds are that if you had access to all that stored information you'd outstrip Einstein. But you don't, or you wouldn't be reading this book.

Now, imagine a large valve sitting at the opening between the conscious and subconscious parts of your mind. (No, this is not biologically accurate but it is a good visual illustration for those of you with strong creative triggers.) When that valve dilates you are capable of effective access to stored knowledge and wisdom. When it closes up you are borderline village idiot. Unless you are truly superhuman you will have suffered from this affliction many times in your life, drying during a presentation, stumbling over your own phone number or being unable to recall the date of your mother's birthday. Some facts are stored in the subconscious so stubbornly that it is impossible to dredge them up at all, ever. You may use your house alarm code number several times a day but be unable to remember it consciously. Many actions, like changing gear when driving or playing notes on a piano, are performed subconsciously.

But why is it that simple and well-known information can escape us on occasion? Why will that fact then pop into your head the minute you no longer need it?

Two things that prevent a free-flow of information and knowledge from the subconscious to the conscious brain are anxiety and stress.

Have you ever taken part in a general knowledge quiz? Pressure and tension will scupper your memory retrieval system, which is why you often see contestants in team quizzes writhing in agony claiming 'I know this one!', rummaging desperately in their subconscious. But the stakes are too high and the information is locked tight.

The adrenalin high that is induced by the sense of competition will provide a heightened awareness and possibly clarity of focus, but even that advantage will count for nothing once that imaginary valve starts to close down for the night.

So when does your brain pop up with the answer to that question? Once it is too late. Usually just as you are nodding off to sleep that night, or when you wake briefly at 3.00am. Why then and not when it was needed? The answer is simple – you gained access once you were relaxed.

## Quality knowledge recovery

Quality knowledge recovery requires manageable levels of stress and anxiety. Creative thinking needs almost negligible levels. Stress and anxiety put the brain into survival mode, and we're talking life, rather than business survival here. Think of a wild animal fighting out of a corner rather than an entrepreneur using his wits to steer him through a work problem.

## Stress-busting

The stress-induced survival response places both the brain and the body under tremendous pressure.

What was once a life-saving reaction becomes – at least – a nuisance, and – at worst – potentially life-threatening.

Take your everyday fear-inducing situation. Imagine you are being chased by a lion. The conscious brain would register the threat and the body would respond magnificently by rising to the challenge. Your heart would beat faster, making your pulse quicken. Your lungs would start to take in more air and your breathing would get more shallow. Your skin would sweat as part of your cooling system. Digestion would shut off as an unnecessary function under the circumstances. Brain functions would become instantaneous.

All useful stuff, unless the perception that triggered the response was faulty. What happens when it isn't a lion that makes you anxious but the thought of an important business presentation? Or merely the fact that the photocopier's run out of paper? Do you suffer a panic attack? What happens when the brain primed for knee-jerk response is left with little else but childish anger or upset?

## Stress relief

Stress is the 'trend' illness of today, and it is one of the most contagious illnesses around. Blamed as the trigger for many other diseases and denounced as being the cause of massive losses to industry in terms of man hours and therefore money, stress has become so much a part of current business life that to say you don't suffer from it is to suggest you are either work-shy or lacking in commitment.

Symptoms vary and so do ways of coping. Root causes are rarely examined by organisations because they are often along the lines of overwork, unrealistic deadlines, unhealthy workstations and a lack of reward in terms of recognition. Far better to bring in a stress expert for a two-day lecture on aromatherapy and relaxation techniques!

## Pain relief

It is difficult to argue with a 'Stress Consultant' because any questioning of their powers can be put down to your own over-stress. However, if a doctor diagnoses medicine for an illness you will be only too aware whether the prescription is working or not. There is no one great cure-all for stress, though. Merely bringing the subject up in a seminar or training course can be enough to bring on an outbreak in people who had thought they were busy but coping.

To repeat: stress is contagious. Evaluate your own stress and the point at which it begins to be destructive. Look for physical symptoms without becoming a hypochondriac. Monitor your levels of clear-headedness and rational thought.

Over-stress will lead to the survival response in your thinking, ability to concentrate and make decisions, and your emotional responses. In other words, it will make you behave like a bad-tempered toddler. (If you normally and consistently behave like this, though, please don't blame stress, it's you who are the problem.)

Deadlines and controllable pressure can bring on great high-level thinking, but constant levels of over-stress will impair the brain's best creative and productive abilities. When you are under high stress the brain reacts as though it were under physical threat. Imagine asking someone who was being attacked by a crocodile whether they could come up with a solution to the last quarter's financial deficit. Would you act on their advice, even if they were capable of giving it? Or would you prefer to listen to someone who appeared calm and relatively relaxed? But then how much would you value the advice of someone who was too laid back and appeared not to care?

## Peak arousal

Your ideal stress levels for tackling goals will probably be around the 'alert and ready for anything' mark. This will be at peak arousal for business but with the capacity to relax and recover when needed. And if that sounds easy to maintain, take our word for it that it's not.

## The dead zone

Under-stress can produce many of the same symptoms as being over-stressed, which is why it's important to keep up levels of challenge and stimulation. The brain and the body respond best to manageable levels of both. Perception of stress 'triggers' are extremely individual. A captain of industry may thrive on the constant challenges of the job, while someone prone to stress could suffer a panic attack just taking the dog to the vet.

Symptoms of over-stress include:

Headaches
Dizziness
Indigestion
Palpitations
Inability to concentrate
Anxiety
Anger
Sweating
Dry mouth
Panic attacks
Weight loss or gain.

The two key words in stress management are CONTROL and PERCEPTION. Loss of control over a situation will heighten feelings of pressure and stress. Faulty perception of the stress triggers will induce a magnified response to stimuli, in terms of both body and brain function.

Another phenomenon of the stress syndrome is the Martyr Response. If you are stressed you will find yourself increasingly unable to delegate. People under pressure begin to absorb even greater burdens. Paradoxically, the stressed person will seek greater and greater levels of challenge.

Relaxation in private life becomes impossible. They will engineer situations where they have to work late or return from holiday to manage an urgent task.

## Managing stress

These two words have to be a bit of a joke, and yet how many of us strive for stress management? The idea that you should be doing something about your own stress levels before it's too late is enough to induce a fit of panic on its own.

Current thinking in the field of medicine seems to imply that most things that go wrong with us are somehow our own fault. Positive Attitude is the great dividing factor between recovery or relapse, as though death is a natural by-product of laziness or indifference.

One of the first steps to coping with stress and powering towards better physical shape is to get off the guilt trip. Guilt – the culprit yet again – is a strange emotion. It makes us stressed but it also makes the things or actions that trigger the guilt somehow more attractive to us.

Eating a bar of chocolate is – for most of us – a wonderful, life-enhancing experience. There are fewer things in life that bring out messages of such instant gratification from our bodies. This is not an enjoyment that has to be learnt or acquired, your taste buds were probably entranced from the word go, unlike things like smoking and drinking for which you had to overcome barriers like nausea, choking, and possibly even disgust before you could get to any enjoyment. And yet we will often feel guilty about eating that chocolate. Result? Raised stress levels and a feeling that 'Now I've had one I may as well eat the whole box.' Enjoyment levels reach zero while guilt levels rocket.

So – the message is clear: if you want to lower your overall levels of over-stress you need to stop feeling guilty about it. Did you ask for all that work? Did you actively encourage the pressure? Did you want to feel as you do now?

## Kill or cure

No cures are guaranteed, either. Don't feel guilty because you're not throwing yourself into flotation tanks and yoga positions with abandon. Chanting, breathing exercises, aromatherapy candles and joss sticks may work for some, but they can drive others wild. Prescribed holidays or 'breaks' can turn a happy workaholic feral. Whale sounds and rainforest tapes can be the final straw that makes the one remaining healthy brain cell go ping.

Look at the alternatives and try things *you* like the sound of. Tapestry, pottery classes, playing heavy metal full blast, painting your partner with chocolate, laughing at a funny movie; if it works for you and causes no one else grief then go for it.

We are each of us marginally more affected by different stimuli, being either:

Aural
Visual
Kinaesthetic
Tactile.

A visual person may well respond to the pictures on television or flicking through a glossy magazine, while the aural types may prefer the right music or a soothing relaxation tape to calm them down.

Just avoid the following when you're searching for a stress cure:

Smoking
Drinking too much
Drugs
Overeating
Competitive sports (exhaustive but non-competitive is better for stress-reduction. Competing – even with yourself – can be stressful)
Too much caffeine.

## Touch

Most of us are tactile creatures, we use self-touch as a method of relaxation, even at work. Watch fellow workers during a meeting or even at their desks. Most will be fiddling with hair, jewellery or watch-straps. This is a self-calming strategy as each touch reminds the subconscious of a time when the body was relaxed.

Cigarettes can be hard to quit – not just because of the nicotine addiction, but because the actual action of smoking and the touch involved reminds the smoker of a time when they were relaxed, thereby stimulating similar feelings.

You can invent your own stress-touch, making it an action that is workplace-friendly, e.g. rubbing the tip of a finger or an earlobe. Do this action whenever you are relaxed and it will eventually become a relaxation trigger for you when you begin to feel stressed.

## Balance

Control is a vital ingredient of over-stress, or rather a lack of it. When you feel your life and time is being controlled externally your stress levels will usually increase. It is important to your stress perception levels that you begin to take mental control of your life. *You* make all the decisions, even though you may not be too keen on the options. Even doing nothing is a decision in itself.

Become responsible for your own actions and decisions. All are taken as a result of your own evaluation of the risks and the consequences.

Never be fooled into believing that this is a small or meaningless step. It isn't; it's one of the most important leaps of conscious thinking you can ever take.

## Stimulus – response

External events do not control our lives and our emotions if we classify them as stimulus. The response to that stimulus is largely up to you. You may not be in control of the stimulus but – in most cases – you are in some way in control of your own response. One person's disaster is another's temporary hiccup. One word of cutting criticism can cause some to give up altogether and spur others on to greater achievement.

Bad things happen. Yet we all know people who have achieved success against every odd life could throw at them. And others who quit and go running for the hills at the first sign of a set-back. The choice will ultimately be yours.

## Charting trouble

One good way of dealing with intolerable stress is to make a stress log for a week.

## Work page 7

**Stress Log**

Chose a time when your life is at its most normal and compile a simple graph to illustrate how stressed or relaxed you felt at what time. Be as honest as possible in your evaluation of your feelings. Just because you were busy or under pressure at a certain time doesn't mean that the result was stress. You may have enjoyed the urgency of the task. That children's party with twenty screaming kids may have been fun for you. Stress triggers are personal. Judge by your *feelings*, rather than your thoughts.

The graph should be easy and quick to compile and – if you feel it is revealing some real clues to your stress patterns – you may like to keep it going for longer than a week. Once you understand the triggers, any potential cures or solutions can become clear.

Look at the highest points on the graph, then answer the following questions:

> What exactly made your stress levels increase at those points?
> Was it due to a real situation or an imagined one?
> Did a person or some people cause the surge?
> Was it due to their actual behaviour or to what you thought their behaviour might be?
> Was the surge due to irrational fear or annoyance or a feeling that you couldn't cope at that time?

If so:

> Did you cope?
> Did you solve the problem or deal with the situation effectively?
> Did anything about your behaviour make the situation worse?
> Could you have done anything to make the situation better?
> How would you have handled the same situation or person if you had been calm at the time?
> Could you have avoided the situation altogether?

## Cut and run

Avoidance is a problem. However, avoiding stress by maintaining a pressure balance in your life is OK. If you are under immense pressure at work it makes sense to put off tiling the roof at the weekend. But just avoiding a situation you find stressful may be less helpful than you think. Sitting worrying passively about a problem can just worsen it. When stress really kicks in the triggers can become disproportionate. Getting rid of some of the most obvious stress triggers may work or it may not. If the stress response has been part of your life for a long time you may find it will trigger in exactly the same way over more trivial events once the greater ones have been removed.

This – of course – is hugely depressing. You could throw in the towel on your break-neck corporate lifestyle and jet off to live forever on some tropical beach only to discover that you are driven just as crazy by the sound of the crickets at night.

Here are some simple solutions for reducing stress. You may be able to do all, some, or none of them:

1. Create balance. Be kind to yourself when you are under pressure. Understand that you can cope but that you will have to take it easy in another part of your life.
2. Don't be a martyr. Delegate. Let some things drop. Allow yourself to make a mistake now and again.
3. Take breaks. Not just holidays (they can actually induce stress) but breaks from your work during the day. Have a lunch hour and get out of the building. Avoid working late hours unless it is absolutely necessary. Don't feel guilty about walking out on time.
4. Work on your perception of the stress triggers. Get life into perspective. Look at your life as a whole. Take control again. Steer it back into the right direction.
5. Invest some time in investigating more practical methods of reducing stress symptoms. Breathing exercises, massage, aromatherapy – if you think it might work for you then give it a go.

## Able-bodied

You don't have to be fit and healthy to be successful, but it can certainly help. Energy is a vital ingredient in goal-achieving, and energy levels are at a premium when you are meeting your body's requirements of sleep, nutrition and exercise.

There is no need to be a purist.

There is also no need for you to use this healthier regime as an excuse for prevarication. Once you have decided on your goals you should get stuck into your work plan as soon as possible.

Don't wait until you have lost three stone/quit smoking/run five marathons before you start, or you'll probably find you'll be waiting forever.

Fuel your body effectively. If you are a junk food fan start switching to healthier options.

So what exactly is healthy eating? Nutritionists disagree over nearly every piece of advice meted out, but a sensible guideline would be:

Moderate portions
Low intake of fats, sugar and salt
Fresh, rather than processed, food
Moderate alcohol consumption
Fresh fruit and vegetables
A combination diet, ensuring all the basic nutrients.

Exercise and a healthy diet need to be seen as a reward rather than a punishment, which is why it's important that neither becomes boring. No one is asking you to enthuse wildly over a lentil casserole or to bound skittishly around a gymnasium if neither is your thing. Find things you *do* enjoy doing and eating. Start small and – if you find you like it – notch up. This is not 'all or nothing' stuff. If you set about your diet or exercise with evangelical zeal, and either or both are a new experience for you, you'll find that recurring problem with guilt if you do fall from grace. Your mental attitude is as important to your goals as your physical shape so you need to avoid a feeling of failure if you pig out on a pizza or forget to go running because it's started to rain.

These things are not crimes. Just learn to treat your body with as much respect as possible, that's all. This will help endorse the idea that you are special and important, vital to your self-esteem.

## Quitting

Oh, and by the way, don't forget to give up smoking. It's not clever and it's not funny. Quit now. Suck your thumb instead if you have to. That way you may look stupid but at least you'll still be alive.

## You look how you feel and feel how you look

Which brings us on to the next point: LOOKING GOOD.

Take yourself off to a mirror and have a long hard look. What is the message you see from the figure standing there? Does he/she look confident and inspired? Is this a creature of energy and passion or a walking apology? How does it market itself via its dress, posture and expression?

You may argue that looks are irrelevant, in which case you'd be wrong. Your visual image is a statement that you make, both to yourself and to the world around you. Success or lack of it can be affected by a negative visual image. Try a very basic exercise: sit hunched in your chair with your arms folded across your chest and try saying: 'I feel wonderful, positive and optimistic.' Now pull yourself upright and smile. Try saying: 'I'm a real loser. Everything I do goes wrong.'

### Mood swings

Visual image can be a mood-changer. Smiling, for instance, is said to cause a physical chain reaction that actually results in making you feel better. Constant and irrelevant smiling will make you look like the village idiot, but encouraging yourself towards a genuinely cheerful expression at appropriate moments can have a positive psychological effect.

You may discover you are frowning a lot of the time without being aware of it. Did you ever catch sight of yourself unexpectedly in a mirror and wonder who the miserable old dog was?

'Fraught' is the expression many of us wear in repose. Raise your eyebrows right now. How much effort was that? How much muscular tension have you just relieved?

Humans read and respond to one another's facial expressions. Non-verbal communication forms as much as 55% of the overall perceived message, and your expression will form a large part of that percentage.

Looking like a champion is one of the greatest steps to becoming one. How you look reflects on how you feel. If you look the part you will find it easier to act it.

Analyse and possibly re-create your image as you look at yourself in the mirror. Think of your heroes, people you would consider great achievers. Do they portray themselves looking closed, cautious and apologetic? Straighten yourself if you need to. Avoid negative 'barrier' gestures with your hands and arms. Relax the facial muscles until you find it easy to wear a confident smile of well-being.

Self-esteem is a fragile quality but it can be enhanced in this basic and very easy way. You need to look happy about being in your own skin.

## Body language

Your gestures should imply you respect yourself, your views and your abilities. Study other people who have been achievers in their own fields: Richard Branson, who always seems to be smiling with his head tilted up and slightly to one side in a rather buccaneer style; Nelson Mandela's smile; Sir John Harvey-Jones's flamboyant ties.

All of these people must be sending positive messages of self-esteem to themselves as well as to their audience. They may feel as nervous or lacking in confidence as the rest of us but those visual tricks can be as enhancing to positive mental attitude as Prince Naseem's 'victory roll' over the ropes before a fight has even begun.

## Visual re-creation

As we have seen, mental preparation is vital to your success plan, and visualising future goals as current reality helps your focus. So does looking the part. Re-create yourself as a winner. Take what you want to be and how you want to look and do it now. You may not have the money for that Mercedes car or designer suit but achieve what you can.

This is one of the simplest, easiest and yet most useful steps you can take en route to achieving your success.

Be stylish, well-groomed and contemporary in your image. Get a good, up-to-date haircut. Get rid of drabness and camouflage. Hone in on even the smallest detail, like bags, pens, notepads and shoes. Do they look like the kind of thing a successful person would own? Jettison any clutter. How good do you feel every time you have to root through all those old tissues and junk to find anything in your bag? How enhancing are those old, unpolished shoes? What do you think that ancient, chewed plastic biro tells people – and yourself – about you every time you bring it out?

By streamlining your image you will be doing some important scene-setting, both for yourself and others. No one has to look like a mess. Many great actors prepare for a role by paying attention to the smallest of details, like wearing appropriate underwear for a period part even though it will never be visible to the audience! Only this new, successful persona you are adopting isn't going to be an act, it will be the new you. Therefore it is even more important you get the look totally right, down to the smallest detail.

Keep outfits simple and stick to the motto that 'less is more'. Your dress can become armour that you use to face the world, but avoid the power dressing look of the 1980's. Find colours that suit you and – even more importantly – suit the way you feel. Colours can affect mood quite dramatically. When you try an outfit on make sure you feel, as well as look, good in it.

## Creating a character

There is room for flamboyance and eccentricity in your successful image, but only if it is a true reflection of your character. People who try to dress 'interestingly' usually end up looking silly.

Flamboyant touches should be a symptom of the real you, not a ruse to create something that isn't there. Suddenly dyeing your hair pink or having your tongue pierced will look more like a cry for help if your normal image is staid. However, even if you are staid you could try stretching yourself gradually, and hopefully a zestier personality might be unleashed.

## A quick guide to dress codes for success

### Try:

### 1. A perfect fit

Even an expensive suit will look cheap if it fits badly. Few people outside the fashion industry have a good eye for a perfect fit, which is why manufacturers gleefully sell us the 'one size fits all' outfit. In fact it usually fits nobody. If we can get into it we will buy it, though. If you've already made that mistake, or eaten your way to a larger size, take the outfit off to a tailor and get it altered accordingly. A good fit will enhance your shape, whatever size you are. Nothing should be tight or straining at the seams. Ankles and wrists should never protrude. Buttons should be buttonable even if you intend leaving the jacket undone.

The answer is not to purchase tents or 'it grows as you do' designs. These garments challenge even the greatest shape to look good in them. Blankets and throw-overs are designed to cover and conceal and if your outfit looks like either you are hiding when you should be centre stage.

### 2. Well-made clothes

This is not the same thing as expensive clothes. Costly garments can be badly made and vice-versa. Study any potential purchase for bad stitching, pulling or any inability to hang or drape correctly. Drape is important to a good look. Some fabrics have an inability to do anything of the kind and you end up looking like the outfit is wearing you, rather than the other way round.

### 3. Cared-for clothes

When you have bought your outfit remember to look after it. Business suits, in particular, tend to be subjected to abuse. Jackets are hung over the back of the chair at the start of the day and leant on regularly. Dry-cleaning is intermittent. Pockets get used like carrier bags until the suit is stretched out of all recognition. Wire hangers are used in the wardrobe. Not even the best outfit can live through that type of constant battering.

### 4. Not looking too self-conscious

Avoid looking too clever. Items should co-ordinate, but not too many should match. An easy rule for bad co-ordinators is no more than one pattern and no more than two colours in any outfit. If in doubt keep it simple. Leave layered and more complicated co-ordinations to the style gurus.

### 5. Not shouting from the rooftops

Funny ties and socks should be made illegal in business. What people do in their own time is up to them. Homer Simpson may be funny but wearing him on a tie doesn't make you amusing too. Be interesting in subtler ways. Fashionable, slightly off-the-wall frames for your specs, for example. A more challenging haircut. A discreet tattoo. Unusual nail varnish. Something that speaks without shrieking.

### 6. Good accessories

A better investment sometimes than the garments themselves. Always be a class act with bags, belts, shoes, pens, etc. No need to spend a fortune, just get the best quality you can afford. Clean shoes are vital. Take a pair to change into if your route to that interview/meeting/conference/the office is liable to inflict grime and scuffs.

(If it is within your budget, treat yourself to a manicure. Good nails give as positive a look as well-polished shoes and the actual act of getting the manicure will make you feel pampered and important.)

## Change for change's sake

From the first day you started to take control of your own appearance you have been making choices of taste that reflect what you consider to be 'you'. When did you last challenge these choices? How long has it been since you last indulged in a bit of serious image re-engineering? When you go into a clothes shop do you make a bee-line for the usual departments, choosing similar outfits that are in keeping with your normal look?

Change for change's sake can give your brain a self-perception kick-start that can work wonders for your positivity. Changing your hair parting, shaving off a beard or wearing patterned tights may not be a quantum leap in your behaviour, but it will push you gently in the right direction.

Challenge tastes that have been acquired for no logical reason. Try different foods. Wear a different look in clothes. Read something you would not normally pick from the bookshelves or listen to a type of music that is at odds with your own preferences.

Holidays refresh and inspire us for precisely this reason, because we have stepped into an alien lifestyle. The change can alter your thinking: until you return home and settle back into your normal patterns, that is. The concept of change will be dealt with in a later chapter but experiment with a small step in your appearance at this stage.

Making subtle alterations to the way you look can result in a heightened feeling of optimism and positivity.

## POSITIVE SELF-TALK

I am self-encouraging, not self-critical

I admire, not envy, the success of others

There is no such thing as a wrong idea

I value myself and my own success

The criticism of others is opinion, not fact

Luck is only one aspect of success

There are at least a hundred ways around every hurdle

Moaning is not one of them

## Review and work plan

**1.** List Towards and Away From emotions.

**2.** Study and begin to manage your own stress. Begin to build balance into your life.

**3.** Create a stress log to see areas of risk and improvement.

**4.** Monitor your levels of physical well-being. Rid yourself of bad habits, like smoking and over-eating. Start to treat yourself with respect and admiration. Take exercise.
Get enough rest, fun and sleep.

**5.** Work on looking good. Create rotas to ensure enough time is spent on your visual image. Let your dress, posture, walk and facial expressions all reflect your desired sense of well-being, status and state of mind. LOOK successful.

# CHAPTER 5

# Time management & delegation

> 'The difference between success and failure is so minuscule it's almost like tossing a coin.
>
> 'It's like the differences between the nuances of shades of grey.'
>
> **Huw Griffiths – Senior Lecturer on Social Work, University of Ulster**

One of the biggest barriers that people have to achieving success is lack of time – not only to think about what they want, but creating sufficient time to *achieve* what they want. We once spoke to a busy professional couple who were desperate to move house but could not create enough time in their hectic schedules to look for what they wanted. Arguably you could say that they just didn't want it enough, or simply didn't have enough foresight and vision to move from their current situation to make that change. In that instance their problem was that they felt they could not delegate and trust others with the tasks that they were working on themselves to create the time to make the move.

How often have you found yourself wanting something, only to discover you are unable to make any time to get what you want, or even have the time to think about what you need? It is a known fact that most of us can spend our lives being busy achieving a lot of things, but not achieving anything purposeful. How do you prevent this from happening to you?

## Locking into time

Focus and time locking are key ingredients. It is very easy for you to lose focus about what it is you are trying to achieve. Because there are so many other distractions around, you find that you end up giving a small amount of time to a variety of tasks, hopping from job to job with many interruptions along the way, working on the things you like doing and the things that you are good at, and shelving the one really big important task that you should be getting on with immediately.

## Time logs

To create thinking time it is important to measure exactly how you currently spend your time. Many people happily measure and monitor their finances at the end of the month to budget and balance the figures. However, how many people fail to calculate where they have spent their time each day/week of the month but continue to complain about being short of time?

Periodical time logging is an important part of measuring your effectiveness, and so is giving yourself an opportunity to decide whether these are the tasks you should be working on. You will then be in a position to link your log to your key area of work and other activities.

Effective time management is essential if you are to create time to achieve your goals and objectives in life. Wasting time is like dropping money down the drain, and very few of us would do that. Simple as it may sound it is important to set yourself a realistic time-scale to achieve specific tasks, dealing with any interruptions along the way.

Decide what task you are going to do, followed by the estimated amount of time you will be spending on it. The time sets the target for completion and helps you focus on the deadline more accurately.

Time logging is also an excellent way for you to assess your effectiveness at that particular task, allowing you to decide how best you could achieve your objective in a smarter way by improving your skills in that area. People who are effective time managers have the ability to focus on what they are trying to achieve, coupled with a time-scale that they have set themselves to achieve that deadline. You can develop effective time management techniques by developing your skills in what you are currently trying to achieve. The skill of time-locking, i.e. focusing on one current task and not thinking about the past or the future, just concentrating on the now, is an essential one.

## Meetings

*Mike writes:* 'I worked with a group of senior directors who requested time management training. I persuaded them all into running time logs on themselves. The result – 80% of their time was spent in meetings, with very little personal time left over... On examining their meetings they found their decision-making skills left a great deal to be desired, because the chief executive wanted agreement on every issue. Time-logging gave them a complete picture of the blockage with their meeting programme, as well as highlighting the leadership issue.'

It might just be that your time log tells you that you are wasting too much time reading or writing reports, using the telephone or attending meetings. This complete picture allows you to redevelop your skills in that particular area, thus becoming more effective.

Good time managers are not usually born that way, they have simply used good techniques to measure where their time goes by time logging, delegating appropriate tasks and always keeping a clear focus about their aims and objectives.

How often have you been pleasantly reading at home only to take a phone call that sends you running around the place sorting someone else's problems out?

How many times have you planned your complete day only to have it scuppered by someone else, or been working well on that budget or report to find yourself getting involved in something else?

## Current time

One good question to ask yourself is: 'Is what I am doing the best use of my time right now?' To achieve your aims and objectives you will have to be conscious about the effects of time wastage. Use the time log module below to discover your own time wastage. Then prioritise your tasks.

## Time Management              Time Log

| Priority | Time | Activity | Length of time | Actions/ How to improve |
|----------|------|----------|----------------|-------------------------|
|          |      |          |                |                         |
|          |      |          |                |                         |
|          |      |          |                |                         |
|          |      |          |                |                         |
|          |      |          |                |                         |
|          |      |          |                |                         |
|          |      |          |                |                         |

You probably have a daily 'to do' list that can span over several pages, either on your computer or in your diary.

Compiling a realistic daily 'to do' list is important. Five or six items is usually a realistic number of activities. Prioritise these under the following headings:

Urgent and important
Urgent not important
Important not urgent
Not important not urgent.

Allocate times against each activity. Clarifying in your mind the difference between urgent and important is essential. There is great benefit in spending your time on pro-active tasks (the future) versus reactive tasks (unforeseen issues). You can easily fall into the trap of not allocating sufficient time for the issues that – for whatever reason – you find appearing in your way for you to resolve. Having a 'to do' list without this space for the unforeseen leaves you in a position where you find yourself eating into the time you had planned for other activities.

## Diaries

The correct use of your diary is also an essential ingredient in being an effective manager of your time. Just using your diary for appointments, instead of using the diary as a daily planner to manage your activities, is an easy trap to fall into.

Make full use of the diary for all your daily activities.

Planning time to think is essential, so allocate space in your diary to do just that. This will enable you to re-engage and plan future activities. Call it creating an appointment with yourself. Take yourself away from the daily hustle and bustle and take time out to think.

> 'Time is like a river
> You cannot step into it twice.'
> *Heraclitus*

## Delegation

You must at some stage have made the statement: 'It's quicker to do the job myself than to delegate the task to someone else.' This response results from confusion between delegation and giving jobs out to other people. Delegation is a vital ingredient if you are to create more time for yourself. Most managers will give out tasks to their team members, but delegation is somewhat different.

True delegation is about agreeing with another individual over carrying out a specific part of your job, so consultation with the other person, agreement, and training to perform the task are all key considerations. It is also important to remember that you delegate authority and responsibility, but not accountability. That means that if the work is screwed up you are still accountable for the outcome. Scary stuff. However, provided you have delegated the task in the right manner, there won't be a problem.

Remember that delegating isn't just about delegating downwards. It is always possible to delegate upwards and across in an organisation. You can also delegate tasks outside the workplace.

The six stages of delegation are:

1. Deciding what to delegate.
2. Deciding whom to delegate to.
3. Consulting and agreeing.
4. Discussing the necessary support or training.
5. Informing other people of level of authority.
6. Continuing monitoring and support.

## Priorities

It is very easy to find yourself doing things without questioning the purpose. You should always be aware of the importance and the urgency of any specific task. Take time now to reflect on your activities and ask yourself a few simple questions:

Tick or cross any of the following:

Am I happy with the way my time is currently allocated? ☐
Do I constantly work long hours? ☐
Do I take work home? ☐
Do I need to change or raise my game to another level? ☐
Have I clearly defined priorities at work? ☐
Have I clearly defined priorities out of work? ☐

Most of us operate at a level far lower than our real capabilities, not really fulfilling our true potential. Delegating specific tasks allows you to look towards greater and better objectives for the future, raising your standards and your sights. Be more specific about your needs and develop others towards those goals by delegating.

## Turning work down

Having the ability to say 'no' will be essential for you to succeed as an effective time manager. We all find ourselves saying 'yes' to things we know we haven't got time to work on, from managers, colleagues, customers and friends. The ability to say 'no' in the right manner is important, using the correct tone of voice and body language.

That sounds all very well and good until your manager gives you another task to achieve on top of everything else. Therefore if you intend using the 'no' word, make sure you really cannot take the job on and then look for other options that you can possibly negotiate on. For example, you can get the other person to help you prioritise by saying: 'Yes I can do that, however, it will mean leaving that particular job.'

Adopting a confident style in life is important, and that means standing up for yourself and being in control about what YOU want and what you expect to happen. Developing a confident style is an area to practise.

Behaviour can range from passive to aggressive and even manipulative. Each of these behaviours can be appropriate to achieve your goal, though, so don't assume assertiveness is always the best option.

Retaining your focus is important for clarity of purpose. A good example of clarity of purpose can be related to groups of individuals versus teams. Give a group a specific task with a deadline and some constraints and they bond incredibly well into a team, usually due to the fact that they are focusing on those constraints and deadlines.

We have observed many business groups that failed to get on with each other or achieve their goals at work, yet when given a specific task, with a specific deadline, they all worked well together, achieving their objective, once some of the more personal minor issues were sorted.

## Team goals

Remember that to achieve your objective, teamwork may be a key ingredient. To reach your objective as an individual is one thing, but working as an effective team member is a completely different ball game. The ability to bring something to the party and be a good member of any team will be an asset.

## Time spent deciding

The decision-making process starts at the outset when you have to decide what you want.

A great deal of time can be lost in the process of decision-making. Decision-making is about making the right choices, with the prime objective of having the ability to select the best alternative. This means you have to take stock of a specific set of criteria on either a grander or smaller scale and arrive at a decision.

As the set of criteria becomes larger so does the difficulty in deciding. No doubt you have at some time had difficulty arriving at any one decision, let alone the right one. There can be something nice about finding only one option available with no choice to make, although the decision then is based on: 'Do I have it or not?' or 'Shall I go there or not?' You will need, therefore, to weigh up all the characteristics of whatever you are making the decision upon. When you think about it, you are taking hundreds of decisions every day, from what to wear or eat, to what route to take to a meeting or conference.

Your ability to take decisions can be hugely affected by the level of stress you are under at a particular time, so avoid taking important decisions when you feel your stress levels are high.

Life will always be about multiple choices. You might find yourself questioning the decision you have taken after the event, asking yourself: 'Was that the right thing to do? What if I'd made the other choice, what would have been the outcome?'

This is similar to the process of negotiating. With negotiating, there is always an element of doubt over whether you have achieved the best deal. You never really know if the person you're negotiating with over price would have lowered it, while they never know if you wanted the trade so much you would have paid full price. That element of self-doubt will always be an issue, but convincing yourself that it was the right decision is important for the sake of your stress levels.

There are many types of models around to help in the

decision-making process. One model – known as a compensatory model (see diagram) – is based on listing the criteria and giving each a weighting. This type of model does in part allow you to look at a far larger range of criteria, allowing you to calculate the final figure and take the right decision based on pure maths.

## Compensatory model

### An example, based on evaluation and weighting procedures

DECISION INVOLVED: CHOSING BETWEEN HOUSE 'A' AND HOUSE 'B'

|  | Location | Garden | Parking | Neighbours | No. of bedrooms |
|---|---|---|---|---|---|
|  | x 10 | x 7 | x 3 | x 9 | x 5 |
| HOUSE 'A' |  |  |  |  |  |
| HOUSE 'B' |  |  |  |  |  |

Make a comparison between house 'A' and house 'B' by adding the allocated weighting for each of the headings selected and totalling the scores. The best decision is the highest score.

*Mike writes:* 'When I bought my Morgan motor car it met the specifications on colour, model, interior design, condition and mileage. The only decision to take was whether I could live with the disc wheels instead of wire spoke wheels, which I saw as a minor compromise. After many hours of deliberation I made the decision.'

Not all of you will work in such a logical manner and most of you will be working with the so called non-compensatory models (Reed 1982), where things are thrown out for not meeting one or two specific criteria. For instance: 'The second-hand car meets the specification I want, but I don't like the colour.'

Your ability to make decisions will be weighted towards the scale of the decision. Deciding which brand of cereal to buy is far easier than which home to purchase. Obvious as it may sound, the effects are far greater, and therefore it requires more time to establish the correct decision. Making small decisions can be easily done. It's the bigger picture decisions that are the ones that really test you, especially if they affect other people, as in a company restructure with all its associated problems.

It's also vital to consider what the effect would be if you got the decision wrong. What problems would you face? Taking this approach or using visualisation techniques may help you realise that it is no big deal if you do get some of the smaller decisions wrong, so go for it.

Time will always be the critical factor when it comes to taking decisions affecting your research into choices. You may wish to seek advice from other people or one specific individual whose decision you would respect. If the decision is marginal, for instance, 'Shall I paint the room blue or green? I like both colours', then just toss a coin. The fact that you like them both will mean it doesn't matter which way the coin falls, but at least it will help you decide. Very often when the coin does land you find your true decision by wishing it had fallen the other side up, so reverse it, because you've now decided.

Avoid dithering over decisions. The longer you take the more stress you put yourself under. Yes, it is important to take all the time you have, but delaying the process only makes it worse. Think about a time when you spent ages deciding about something and remember how you felt, and the euphoria after the decision had been taken.

There are some key areas in taking decisions:

- Consider there is a decision to take.
- Consult anyone affected or people who may affect your decision.
- Crack the decision – take it – believe in it.
- Communicate to those affected.
- Check that the decision is implemented, in place and working.

Many decisions allow you to follow this process through. However, there are occasions when – because of time or situation – a different approach may be needed. If the building is on fire or the ship is sinking then standing there consulting may not be the best approach! You may have to get on with the job in hand and explain and analyse later.

Good decisions are easily explained to those affected. It's when you cannot explain your decision that it's time to change it, and be prepared to admit: 'I got this one wrong.'

---

### Review and work plan

1. Run a time log over a short period.
2. Compare allocation of time against specific tasks.
3. Analyse and develop an action plan.
4. Compile simple 'to do' lists at work and home.
5. Prioritise tasks into urgent and non-urgent.
6. Make the most of your diary by scheduling specific tasks.
7. Decide on issues to delegate and adopt the delegative procedure.
8. Learn to say 'no' to non-specific tasks.
9. Be decisive about decision-making. Always carry a coin for marginal decisions.

# Learning

> 'You don't know what you don't know. There is always something else out there, so unless you keep going you'll never find it.
> *You can get satisfaction out of every situation by thinking positively.'*
>
> 'One of the greatest things that I learned in life is the importance of self development and the power of learning itself.'
>
> **Mike Watson – Director, O.M.D Associates Ltd**

Learning is a combination of knowledge, skills, attitude, behaviour and confidence, with a *change* in behaviour being one of the key expectations and definitions of learning.

There is little or no point increasing knowledge and skill if the attitude is not right or confidence is lacking. In fact you could argue that increasing the information and skills level in an individual whose attitude is flawed or who lacks confidence just compounds the problem. Some good examples of confidence linked to learning can be related back to the time when you learnt to ride a bike or swim. Without the essential ingredient of confidence the objective of swimming or cycling would not have been achieved.

However, if you have strong motivation and desire to master new skills your objective is usually achieved. You may have found that the motivation to ride a bike came from the fact that everyone else could ride one and you would get left behind if you couldn't. Or you may have overcome your fear of the water when you found yourself sitting on the edge of the pool alone with everyone else splashing around in the water having fun.

To learn anything you must keep an open mind. Have you ever tried to teach anyone who is constantly telling you they can't learn or take in the subject or instructions?

The mental state of preparedness required for effective learning was best described by Olympic medallist Duncan Goodhew. He told his audience that their minds must be like a parachute, which only works when it's open.

With motivation linking to achievement, you soon find that when you learn something new you become more motivated towards further learning. Keeping that statement in mind is itself an excellent motivator.

When you approach a variety of learning situations, new topics or experiences, it is very easy to pre-judge the amount of knowledge you already have and shut your mind off to the new information being passed on to you.

*Mike writes*: 'I recently attended a seminar with a very senior colleague, who had pitched up to the event with the attitude: "I know this stuff, I've heard it all before." Her behaviour and attitude during the event reflected a closed mind. It was not until a number of weeks later that she realised that much of the information discussed at the event was indeed useful. What had caused the behaviour in this particular instance was a lack of initial respect for the presenter and his style, which shut down my colleague's mind and her overall approach to learning.'

Your approach to a subject may be less arrogant, however, and you may suffer more from lack of confidence in your own ability to take information on board.

How often have you told yourself: 'I'm no good at maths', or 'I will never be able to swim or pass my driving test'? Creating negative thinking will have a huge impact on how you learn.

You will know that learning is based on experiences and practices, which eventually change our behaviour. It is also important for you to understand learning in the broader context of life, instead of merely relating it back to your school days, when much of your learning was based on study and very little else. What you will find is that when we think about learning in the broader sense we learn very quickly.

When there is an element of danger, for instance, you learn quickly. If you hold your hand over a candle it burns you, and consequently you learn not to do so. If you touch a bare electrical wire and get a shock, you very quickly learn that it's not a good thing to do. It's almost as if the effect has such an impact on the learning experience that you never forget the lesson.

## POSITIVE SELF TALK

My energy is charged by my enthusiasm

I never stop learning

The scope of my potential is limitless

I never waste energy on complaining

I create my own success

My creativity, positivity and open-mindedness are what give ideas the freedom and space to fly towards light

My success is based on real strategies and positive thinking

I give myself praise and rewards

I create my own barriers to that success

## Mistake-based learning

A major part of learning, then, can come from making mistakes. We're sure that when moving from the current reality towards your objective, mistakes will be made. Therefore, it is essential that you condition your thinking and attitudes towards mistakes.

If you did all of your maths homework at school and scored ten out of twenty, invariably there would be an element of disappointment. You would look at why you got ten questions wrong, with a view to learning what mistakes you had made in your calculation. If you fail to review, you invariably make the same mistakes at exam time, leaving you with a poor result.

It is also important – as mentioned previously – to learn from success, something which we are not good at in the UK. The doom and gloom of an accident or major disaster usually sparks off a major enquiry to find out who did what, where, when and how, usually with the purpose of blaming instead of learning from the mistake. Analysing why so many oil tankers don't sink and do sail through difficult waters might prevent the odd one from sinking, instead of holding a massive enquiry after a disaster has occurred.

## Learning from success

The possibility of learning from success is enormous. Could you imagine drafting a check-list based on success, rather than drafting one after a disaster has occurred?

*Mike writes*: 'During my days as an engineer, most of the learning came after an accident had occurred. Although it would be unfair to say that people weren't trained in safety procedures, due to time, pressure, lack of sleep and – in some cases – the desire to cut corners, the motivation to override the previous learning behaviour existed.'

Motivation to learn is essential. You will have a variety of motives for wanting to achieve your objective.

*Mike writes*: 'My motivation to pass my driving test at the age of 17 was triggered by the fact that my pals were sitting around the corner with their bags packed ready to go on holiday. Failure to pass meant no holiday. With a strong sense of purpose and commitment to my pals I passed my test, and we set off on our trip. Had the driving instructor been aware of this it might have been a good learning experience for him and his future test applicants.'

You can learn if the motivation to do so is strong enough, coupled with clarity of purpose.

Think of a time when you started a new job and found yourself having to learn a whole raft of new things, like colleagues' names and procedures. Ask yourself what your motivation to learn these things was. Possibly to survive, impress, or to be as good as you were in your previous job. Or it might have been the fact that it was new, exciting and, above all, of interest to you.

## Teaching success

Learning is affected by the interest developed by the person teaching you.

*Mike writes*: 'I excelled at maths at the age of 14 because my maths teacher, father and grandfather made the subject meaningful. It was not just the calculations that were of interest, but, more importantly, how I would put them into practice as an engineer.'

You won't want to learn mathematical equations if you are never going to apply them in your life. Your commitment, motivation and sense of purpose for acquiring and absorbing the information will be nil, giving you the attitude that it is pointless learning the stuff.

Having a reason to learn anything is essential. Without purpose there is little or no motivation.

*Mike writes*: 'I once had several flying lessons as I fancied myself as a pilot. With no *real* reason for doing it I soon found myself quitting and spending the money on something less costly and more purposeful.'

## Quitting

Knowing when to quit is also important at all stages of learning. 'This is not for me' can be a valued response. Making someone learn to be a good presenter is pointless if they are going to find the experience too daunting.

Deciding what you want to learn *and why* is critical, although you may have a natural hunger for learning, hoovering up everything in your path with ease and intent.

A great deal has been written about preferred learning styles. Think of an example of something you have recently learnt and ask yourself the following questions:

'What motivated me to learn this?'

'How did I feel at the time?'

'What mistakes, if any, did I make during the learning process?'

'What did I do well?'

'What would I do differently if I were to go through the same learning experience?'

Learning is a personal experience, therefore you will need to compile your own personal list under the heading:

*What works for me — what enables me to learn?*

1.  ................................................................
    ................................................................

2.  ................................................................
    ................................................................

3.  ................................................................
    ................................................................

4.  ................................................................
    ................................................................

5.  ................................................................
    ................................................................

6.  ................................................................
    ................................................................

7.  ................................................................
    ................................................................

8.  ................................................................
    ................................................................

9.  ................................................................
    ................................................................

10. ................................................................
    ................................................................

For learning to take place it is essential that there is a degree of concentration.  Concentration span will vary from situation to situation and person to person. List five things that help you concentrate:

1.  .................................................................................
    .................................................................................

2.  .................................................................................
    .................................................................................

3.  .................................................................................
    .................................................................................

4.  .................................................................................
    .................................................................................

5.  .................................................................................
    .................................................................................

Much research has been done on classical conditioning. One of the best known pieces of research was done by Ivan Pavlov, when a bell was devised to ring just before a dog's food was brought into a room. A ringing bell does not usually make a dog's mouth water, but after hearing the bell ring many times just before getting fed, Pavlov's dogs began to salivate as soon as it sounded.

It was as if they had learned that the bell signalled the appearance of food, and their mouths watered even if no food followed.  Many other such experiments have taken place since to learn about classical conditioning.

## Sweet motivations

Often the motivation to learn can be a reward or benefit. Try telling a six year old that they can have a bag of sweets if they recite their ten times table, and then observe the motivation to learn. Children have enormous learning potential which can be captured by teachers and influenced by family and friends. One of the great difficulties when teaching children to learn arises when it appears to be learning for learning's sake.

Learning will play a major part in achieving your objective. Without self development you will not grow.

## Motivation rewards

Rewards have always been good motivators when linked to learning. Many organisations reward people, not just for their knowledge and skill, but also when they apply these skills, encouraging and developing learning. Self development has become a key issue within organisations that have fewer opportunities for staff to move up the organisation, ensuring the only opportunities to change roles occur if they move sideways across the organisation. Learning and developing new skills in a fresh area may be the only way to get yourself out of your existing rut, if that's how you feel about it.

A major part of learning may be your ability to make a slight change in your behaviour and – as previously mentioned – taking on knowledge and skill should result in a change in behaviour if you have taken the learning on board.

Research has shown that focusing on the behaviour that you want to achieve is more successful than maintaining a focus on the behaviour you are trying to eradicate. An excellent example to think of would be that instead of trying to be less shy when it comes to mingling at a conference, you could target your behaviour at being more outgoing or sociable.

*Mike writes*: 'An example I took for myself was the very issue of mingling at a conference. I learned to become good at mingling by taking this approach...

'When attending a conference that I was expected to socialise at I used to find someone I knew and talk about things of common interest.

'Now, when attending a conference, I introduce myself to people I do *not* know – ask about their company and their interest in the event. I set myself a target of how many people I can speak to during the day.'

Again, it is important you reward yourself for making this happen.

Take an example for yourself and say what you currently do and then write down what you *should* do. List five rewards for making the change:

1. .................................................................
   .................................................................

2. .................................................................
   .................................................................

3. .................................................................
   .................................................................

4. .................................................................
   .................................................................

5. .................................................................
   .................................................................

Attitudes and behaviours are not always as straightforward as they may seem. Many of our basic attitudes stem from experiences early in life. When children are rewarded with positive encouragement when pleasing their parents, and are punished with disapproval when they displease them, the experience gives them positive and negative attitudes towards future situations.

Attitudes are also formed by the behaviour of parents, teachers, friends and other influential people. The media will also have a huge impact on our attitudes towards a whole range of issues.

It has been proved that you have the ability to tune out from the information thrown at you when attempts to change your attitude occur. One interesting concept is that your attitude is influenced by the source − or credibility of the source − that is trying to affect or influence it. If you have respect and belief in the source, you are more likely to change your attitude.

Attitudes are open to change. However, the reality is that they are very difficult to change. Change in attitude is often not as important as change in behaviour. Often a change in behaviour is followed by a change in attitude.

Take a subject you wish to learn and score your ability out of ten in each of the following areas:

1. *Knowledge*            0.................... 10
2. *Skill*                0.................... 10
3. *Attitude*             0.................... 10
4. *Confidence*           0.................... 10
   equals a *change in behaviour*

You can apply this understanding when you complete your Slope of Achievement analysis in Chapter 14.

---

**Review and work plan**
1. Be confident in your ability to learn.
2. Keep an open mind towards any learning situation.
3. Remember, parachutes only work when they are open.
4. Learn from your successes and evaluate failure – learn from every situation.

# CHAPTER 7

# Creating confidence

'What makes me confident? Being praised. What makes me lack confidence? When someone takes the Mickey.'

**Morgan Edden, aged 14**

'I am the greatest.'

**Mohammed Ali**

*On coping with failure*
'It's important to accept disappointment. Your legs turn to jelly. There is nothing worse than that feeling inside. Things always look better the next day and then you get up and say: "Let's rock and roll".'

**David Mitchell – Chief Executive of The Astron Group**

Of all the problems we've encountered on thousands of training courses, lack of confidence has to be the one that almost every single delegate – without exception – seems to suffer from in one form or another.

Lack of confidence is disabling. It clips your wings and stunts achievement. Self-confidence allows you to shine. Self-belief is vital if you are to realise even one quarter of your potential.

So what is confidence?

You know the feeling of confidence, and you know how you feel on the occasions when you lack it. It can best be described as a state of hope that you need to rely on to produce positive action. Sometimes it is a result of knowledge and experience and sometimes it is more elusive, dependent on intangibles for its presence and growth.

Confidence can be eradicated by anything and nothing: a chance comment or look, a well-aimed criticism, the presence of too many people, glancing into the mirror under the wrong lighting, being self-critical or over-analytical of your own ideas: any or all of these circumstances are enough to bleed your self-confidence dry within seconds.

You will need confidence and self-belief to reach your goals. Without confidence and self-belief success is difficult, if not impossible, to achieve.

Lack of confidence can be the result of the triumph of your subconscious over your conscious mind. When the two are in conflict the subconscious will nearly always win! Take a business presentation. Your conscious mind may remind you that you are well-prepared and knowledgeable about the subject you are going to talk on. Your subconscious may be full of fear, however, constantly reminding you that you hate speaking in public and rehearsing the humiliation that will ensue when it goes wrong. Not only will those subconscious messages lead the charge, they will also make sure they become a self-fulfilling prophesy by creating a state of mind and body that will scupper potential success.

To repeat: most of the barriers that stand between you and success lie in your own mind. We've talked about negative inner dialogues that push you through the door marked 'Failure' before you have even made the effort to try. The truth is that we happily engineer our own downfall before we have even embarked on the journey towards success.

How can you power yourself in the opposite direction, then? How can you create confidence, rather than destroy it? How can you build self-esteem, rather than erode it by negative assumptions?

Hope and belief in a positive outcome are vital. Confidence provides that hope.

Crooked arrows rarely hit their mark. A straight arrow that is pointed towards the target will. Your vision should be one that accepts and expects the best outcome.

**Vital fact**
You need to believe that success is what you deserve.

You should see that your commitment and abilities are strong enough to lead you towards your final goal. You will have natural reservations, of course, but your focus should never really waver. Doubts and barriers should be dealt with as part of your strategy, and this is taken into account when you complete the Slope of Achievement analysis later in the book.

Confidence should never be confused with arrogance. Over-confidence can be destructive to your plans. However, the right levels of confidence will help you create and work on the most effective strategies because you will be relatively unhampered by self-doubt.

## Mentally muscle-bound

If you believe confidence is something you must be born with you are wrong. Confidence is like a muscle, it can be worked on and built up gradually. Only you have to keep working and you have to keep pushing yourself if you are going to improve. The steps to building confidence are easy to describe but less easy to do. It will require some effort from you.

Reading this chapter alone will not be enough to do the trick. You're going to have to go out there and put the ideas into practice.

## Step 1 – become analytical

Be specific about your own fears. Exactly when and where do you most lack confidence? If your answer is 'all the time and everywhere' start with an easier question: when do you feel *most* confident?

Create a list for both, to study recurring themes and triggers, for example:

## Situations where I lack confidence

Public speaking
Speaking up in meetings
Socialising with strangers
Cooking
Mathematical problems
When I talk to someone I am attracted to
Phoning clients
Negotiating a price for goods
Making a complaint.

## Situations where I feel confident

Talking to friends
Relaxing at home
Driving
Doing my normal job
Teaching others
Phoning business colleagues or suppliers
Shopping
Speaking French.

Make your own lists and compare the two. What seems to create your confidence in certain situations and what appears to sap it?

## Situations where I lack confidence

..............................................................................................

..............................................................................................

..............................................................................................

..............................................................................................

..............................................................................................

..............................................................................................

..............................................................................................

..............................................................................................

..............................................................................................

..............................................................................................

..............................................................................................

## Situations where I feel confident

........................................................................................

........................................................................................

........................................................................................

........................................................................................

........................................................................................

........................................................................................

........................................................................................

........................................................................................

........................................................................................

........................................................................................

Think of a specific and recent situation when you felt your confidence drain. Visualise the process. What happened? What switch was flicked to make you feel like that? The effect of that could have been like a trip-out switch on the electricity, disabling the entire system. Analyse the trigger. Ask yourself: 'WHAT TRIPPED THE SWITCH?'

Using this key phrase can encourage you to be objective about your own lack of confidence. It is not going to be used to allot blame, but it will be a vital stage in pre-empting a repeat experience.

By understanding and analysing your confidence levels you can start to raise them in any given situation.

## Potential switch-trippers

### 1. Other people

Obvious but true. These can be strangers or people you regularly see. Good friends rarely trip your confidence but acquaintances and work colleagues can. Family members seem to excel in the art because they know exactly which buttons to press for maximum effect. What is more, they could have inflicted the damage years ago – even before you could speak – as self-esteem is first created in the cradle and then on through childhood.

Even when other people are not critical we can imagine they are. Your Negative Inner Voice will tell you that people are thinking you appear foolish or that you are boring or talking rubbish, even when that is not true. A silent audience of strangers can be even more daunting.

Certain types of people may be intimidating to you. You may find that people in authority sap your confidence. Or arrogant sales assistants. Or aggressive drivers. Or people more confident than you. Or maybe it's just one or two people, like your boss, or your father-in-law.

### 2. Being criticised

Nobody likes criticism and you may find it a major confidence-sapper. Confident people have faith in their own abilities and can take criticism as an alternative opinion. If you lack confidence, however, you will take every critical comment as a death-blow, no matter how many compliments you have already gathered for the same piece of work or performance.

### 3. Being laughed at

One of the greatest fears of the person who lacks confidence is the fear of looking a fool.

*Judi writes*: 'My background is on the catwalk and the good thing about any stage performance is that you quickly learn to lose this fear, mainly because you end up doing something more foolish in front of a large audience than most non-performing people would ever get a chance to achieve. Making a huge fool of yourself in front of a crowd of strangers is peculiarly uplifting and liberating. Some find the laughter addictive and turn to a career in comedy.'

Ask yourself: 'What's the worst thing that can happen in this situation?' Being foolish is rarely life-threatening.

### 4. Uncertainty

You will probably feel more confident in situations you are familiar with. Control breeds confidence, and so does knowledge and experience. Even fear and anxiety can be reduced with regular exposure to the situation that appears threatening. People who feel unthreatened by situations that would faze most of us are usually only confident because either: a) They're used to it, or b) They couldn't care less.

**Reinforcing the certainty, not the uncertainty = confidence.** Get as much knowledge about the situation as you can. Then focus on what you actually know, rather than worrying about what you don't.

### 5. The imagination

Your imagination is a great tool for forging success, but it can also be applied in the opposite direction. Worry destroys confidence, and worry is the result of a badly-programmed imagination. You see everything going wrong. You rehearse the worst. Then you make it happen.

### 6. Stepping into the unknown

To get to confidence and success you're going to have to go through discomfort. New situations may make you lack confidence but it is only by making them less new that you can learn to feel relaxed about them. Take a room full of strangers at a social event. You may have to 'do the room'. However, you may – like most people – have a horror of small talk. You may be allergic to strangers, especially new business clients. Your gravitational pull tells you to find someone you know and stay chatting to them, even though this will never raise your profile or get you new business.

Remember the arm-folding exercise in the Introduction? This is exactly the same experience. You feel uncomfortable but the only way to overcome that feeling and head towards confidence is through discomfort.

**You have to push yourself, and push yourself regularly, to learn confidence. The unfamiliar has to become the familiar, even if it hurts.**

Exercises will help.

Turn to the next page and start to make a pact with yourself. You are going to create a list of daily challenges that will test your self-confidence. These challenges need not be great in terms of effort or size but they will have to hurt to do the job. They will not be physically dangerous or illegal, and will not harm or unduly embarrass anyone else. If you decide to go shopping in a loin cloth, however, don't go with your partner, it is your exercise not theirs!

## List of daily challenges

..................................................................................................

..................................................................................................

..................................................................................................

..................................................................................................

..................................................................................................

..................................................................................................

..................................................................................................

..................................................................................................

Some examples of confidence-training exercises (but only for inspiration, please plan your own):

1. Singing karioke.
2. Asking a stranger for directions.
3. Asking for a pay rise.
4. Bartering in a shop that you think doesn't barter.
5. Walking into a betting shop and placing a bet if you have never done it before.
6. Wearing something a bit daring.
7. Going to a social event and talking to ten new people in an hour.
8. Complaining assertively in a restaurant if the food is not up to expectations.
9. Asking for something that is not on the menu.
10. Disagreeing assertively with someone you find intimidating.

### 7.  Being modest
Modesty is an attractive quality but it erodes confidence. Make another list, then, of all your wonderful personality traits, your successes and achievements, your values and your skills. No negatives on the list please – even self-effacing ones – and then bask in a warm glow as you read the list back to yourself.

### 8. Feeling isolated by shyness

Confidence is an attractive quality as confident people are usually easy company. Lack of confidence, though, can be isolating. You feel you have nothing to offer the gathering and you experience pangs of discomfort. You assume everyone else feels confident in the same situation and that you are alone in your suffering.

The simple fact is that everyone lacks confidence in certain situations and that some become so adept at masking their feelings that you'd never know.

Take the first three letters of CONFIDENCE and you have the secret: for most people it is a con act. They feel exactly the same way that you do – perhaps even worse – but they have learnt to mask their feelings.

### 9. Old experiences

A negative experience can stimulate lack of confidence around anything with similar associations.

Always remember the past has nothing to do with the present unless you give it permission. Each day is a fresh start and you have the opportunity to re-create yourself. Old experiences only haunt you if you let them. Good ones will power you forward but the bad ones needn't drag you back. Learn from your mistakes, but learn in a forward direction.

### 10. Statistics

Stacking the odds against yourself statistically will sap your confidence, e.g. 'Very few women succeed in politics'; 'Thousands of people want to get a book published every year and only a handful are'; 'Your chances of success in that field are very slim'; 'You have little chance of getting a new job after the age of forty.'

All these statements bring good news along with the bad. Turn them around and focus on the positive messages, i.e. 'Some women do succeed in politics and one became Prime Minister of Britain'; 'Several new authors get published every year', etc. Talk yourself up, not down. Which leads us to step two…

## Step 2 – positive programming

As we mentioned in the Introduction, modesty and diffidence are national characteristics in the UK. We are repulsed by the brash and the boastful, so much so that we prefer to talk ourselves down rather than be accused of either.

Now, while modesty is an extremely attractive and laudable quality, it does very little for your self-esteem or sense of potential achievement. We get so adept at the modesty lark that we start to believe it ourselves. Our subconscious starts to store these low self-evaluation statements away as undisputed truth about our own incompetence.

This goes back to the power of the subconscious and the fact that it is a largely non-judgmental storage space. Keep repeating to yourself and others for long enough that you're not very good at something, or that you 'can't' do it, even as a self-effacing joke, and the joke will begin to backfire by becoming reality. These are called Negative Affirmations. Bombard your subconscious with them for long enough and they'll become a self-fulfilling prophecy.

### Inner dialogues

The words you use when you speak have a far-reaching power that is probably much greater than you might think. Some phrases are obviously detrimental: 'I'm just so stupid' being a classic example. But then there are the subtleties, too. Words that provide negative fuel for your potential, like 'try' or 'quite', as in: 'I'm going to try to achieve that goal' or 'I'm quite confident I can do it.' These words may slip into your speech patterns out of habit, you may not even be aware that you've used them. And yet their effect on your perception is long-reaching and destructive.

'Try' is registering failure and courting it even before you've made an attempt. 'Quite' is a diluting word, watering down what could be powerful phrases and statements. Ditto 'kind of', 'sort of' and 'hopefully'.

### Don't programme 'don't'

'Don't' is one of the most useless words to tuck into a sentence as it always translates into the subconscious as 'do'.

Tell a friend in a pub not to turn around because their ex has just walked in and their head will spin 180%.

Warn a child not to drop a valuable plate they are carrying and you may as well get the dustpan out for the bits.

When you want to send yourself a command make sure it's a 'do' one. Point yourself towards what you want to happen, not what you don't.

## The erosion process

Whereas negative statements will erode confidence, so positive ones will help to create and sustain it. It doesn't even matter if you don't believe them to be true. Your subconscious will tend to accept them and respond accordingly, just as it did with the negative ones.

Did you ever have someone ask you if you felt alright because you looked tired or ill? What was the instant effect of that question on your well-being? Didn't you start to feel tired or lethargic, even if you had been glowing a few moments before?

And how about when someone points out that the room is stuffy or the central heating is unbearably high, doesn't that make you feel even warmer than you did? Was there ever a skill that you carried out with competence until the moment someone told you it was difficult?

We are all open to suggestion, especially a negative one. Re-programme yourself by creating positive phrases related to the skills, emotions or state of mind you need to realise your particular goals. This is a technique known as creating Future History, where you take what you desire to be fact and place it in the present tense to help you achieve it.

'I feel calm and in control' is a good repeated phrase to help you overcome moments of stress.

'I am wide awake and raring to go' helps deal with early morning sluggishness.

'I thrive on challenge and change' works on combating the terrors of a new situation.

'I enjoy meeting new people' – if you find strangers difficult to deal with.

## Subconcious saturation

Take whatever you want and saturate your subconscious with the phrase. Persist, even when the negative dialogue tries to step in and tell you you're talking rubbish. Say the phrase out loud and in your own head. Remember that link between the stimulus or event and the attached emotion that settles into your subconscious and can't be overridden by a conscious command? This technique is the most powerful method of uncoupling the two. It may take effect so gradually that you'll barely recognise it's happening, but you will feel your emotions slowly becoming more positive.

This is how you begin to create confidence in the subconscious. Tell yourself you *can* do something, not that you can't. Coach yourself upwards with key phrases like 'Go for it!' or 'You can do it!' Write them down if it helps. Stick them onto the bathroom mirror so that they are the first thing you see when you get up in the morning.

## Step 3 – picture your success

The imagination is a powerful tool. Children learn to handle real-life situations through play-acting and visualising. This is their way of rehearsing success.

As you got older you began using a different technique: rehearsing failure. If there was a situation you were dreading your mind would trawl through the nightmare scenario, seeing all that could go wrong going wrong. Like any other rehearsal, this one was guaranteed to make you more adept at failure because that's just what you had been practising.

## Never waste your imagination in worrying – use it to rehearse success instead

In future make all your mental rehearsals positive ones. See yourself doing well. See things or situations working. Time is a valuable commodity and you should never waste yours by worrying. Use any moments you have prior to a challenging event in positive mental rehearsal.

If you can relax your mind you can create a very fair facsimile of real life. Sit quietly for a few moments with your eyes closed and imagine you are cutting, smelling and finally eating a very sour lemon. The chances are the mental image will have stimulated your saliva glands, just like the real thing.

By seeing in your imagination a situation or event that made you feel relaxed and happy you can alter your mood when you're tense or at a low ebb.

Visualisations are used extensively on the sports fields to create success. A footballer will see the ball going into the net prior to taking a penalty kick, a golfer will see the ball dropping into the hole even when the hole is not visible from the tee.

The same techniques will work in business or everyday life.

## Visualisation warm-up exercise

Try a simple visualisation now. Read the steps through first, then close your eyes and go ahead with your visualisation.

Imagine for the purpose of this exercise that you are facing a real, snow-covered mountain and that you are going to climb to reach the top – this is your goal.

You are now at the base of the mountain about to set off on your climb. You may never have climbed before but you are now trained, fit and confident, full of anticipation and excitement. The sun is warm on your face and lighting up the crags in front of you. Turn your face up into the warm sun and see the peak of the mountain. What you will see when you look up there is your goal, solid and real. You know at this moment that the climb will be challenging but that you will enjoy every stage of it. You are also sure that you will reach your goal at the end of the climb.

Look down at yourself. You are dressed warmly and appropriately. Your clothes are comfortable but able to protect you against the snow. Your shoes are thick-soled and warm. There are spikes on the soles to make slipping or falling impossible. The hood on your head makes you feel protected and safe. On your back is a rucksack with all you will need to sustain you but it is still light enough to make walking easy.

Look at the pure white snow and the beautiful view in front of you. Feel the clear air as it enters your lungs. Savour the sense of anticipation and the emotions you know you will feel once you have reached your waiting goal. Now set off on your journey.

Did you manage to enjoy the scene? Were you able to experience the feeling of well-being, excitement and anticipation? If you found it difficult, practise as often as you have the time and patience.

Once you have tried this visualisation and succeeded with it you can begin to use the same technique on other, real-life goals, injecting positive feelings and emotions just as you did on the mountainside. See yourself winning. See things going well.

There are three main reasons for doing visualisations:

1.  To indulge in positive dress-rehearsals for the key event.
2.  To thereby change the attached and often subconscious emotions. By seeing a situation you find daunting going well you will begin to uncouple the negative feelings and re-attach positive ones.
3.  To become more creative in your strategies for handling situations or planning for objectives. Your mind tends to work in learned patterns, often cancelling out what might be a creative and inspired strategy for no better reason than 'You know it wouldn't work' or 'That's not the sort of thing I would do.' By visualising yourself having already reached your goal you will find your brain is more creative when it is asked the question: 'How did I do that?', rather than the original standpoint of: 'How can I do that?' The barriers to your achievement are no longer there when your view is retrospective. You got there; all you have to do is find out how.

### Picture power

Pictures exert a powerful effect on our behaviour. Help turn goals into reality by seeing them, feeling them, touching them and even smelling them in your imagination.

## Visualisation strategy planner

**1.**

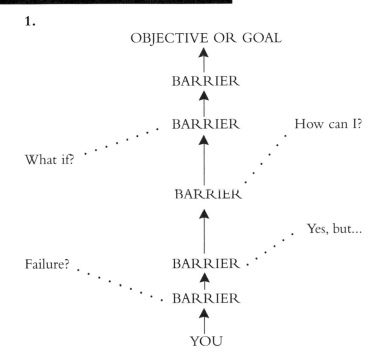

OBJECTIVE OR GOAL

BARRIER

What if? · · · · · · . BARRIER    How can I?

BARRIER

Yes, but...

Failure? · · · · · · · · · BARRIER · · ·

· · · BARRIER

YOU

**2.**

YOU

VISUALISED STATUS

OBJECTIVE OR GOAL

RETROSPECTIVE STRATEGY-PLANNING – HOW
DID I GET HERE? HOW DID I CREATE MY
ACHIEVEMENT?

HOW DID I DO THAT?

## Step 4 – act confidently

Behave and look as though you already have the confidence you desire. Study other people who you think have the confidence you would like to achieve. How do they look? What do they do? How do they sound? What is their body language like? You can even boost your confidence in more extreme cases by pretending in your mind to be that person. Role-playing through another character is a technique many people use, pretending to be Ballesteros when they take that all-important swing in golf, or being a famous singer when they take the mike on karioke night.

Children will often role-play their heroes and this is a technique adults can copy. 'Borrow' the qualities you need. When you are confronted by a challenging situation adopt an ideal persona, as an actor would take on a role.

A room full of strangers can be daunting, especially for the shy. Imagine how a confident, outgoing person would act. Visualise their behaviour and then mimic it. How quickly would they move to the first group? What would they say in introduction? How would their gestures and eye contact be? Would they smile? Would they talk or listen?

## Steeling yourself

Nerves, shyness and even fear can be lessened by a few behavioural tricks. For example, humming, whistling or even quietly singing a cheerful, optimistic tune when you are under pressure can have the effect of turning a situation around. Soldiers would sing as they marched in the First World War. Most of the famous songs of that time appeared to laugh in the face of death. Going into business might not be the same as walking into the trenches but a cheery song might help all the same.

Don't be too serious about your choice of tune. The more ridiculous or lightweight, the more effective it can be. If the thing annoys you as well, so be it. Remember Julie Andrews warbling about her 'favourite things' during a storm scene in 'The Sound of Music'? 'High Hopes' can be equally effective when you're about to give up on an objective, or how about Monty Python's

'Always Look on the Bright Side of Life' to raise a smile when things are going really badly?

A stirring march or TV theme tune can take you striding into a difficult situation when you think you're about to cut and run. If you whistle or hum others will think you are feeling confident and that perception may help you to mask more effectively. Music has been used as a method of inspiring confidence and valour and getting people into battle for centuries. Chose your own theme and use it in times of stress or anxiety.

## POSITIVE WORDS

Unbeatable    Do wonders    Accomplishment

Hit the jackpot    Turn up trumps

Fruitful

Take the prize    Make the grade

Efficient

Do marvels

Profitable    Excel

Rise to the occasion

Romp home

---

### Work plan and review

1. Focus on building confidence and self-esteem.
2. Use positive language and positive self-coaching phrases.
3. Rehearse success through visualisations.
4. Develop your visualisation skills to enable you to achieve enhanced strategy-planning techniques.
5. Role-play your heroes. Create your own theme tune.

# CHAPTER 8

# *Self coaching*

> 'Everyone knows what to do with a kicking horse except the person who owns it.'
>
> **Anon**

Coaching has become one of the essential skills expected of leaders for the next decade. This has been in sympathy with the move away from command and control and 'do as I tell you' styles towards techniques of self-discovery about what to do or how to approach specific issues, thus enhancing self-interest and motivation.

There is a strong possibility that you may have already been on the receiving end of someone coaching you at work. It can, however, be a misconception to assume that everyone enjoys and benefits from the coaching technique. To quote one employee who told his boss: 'Never mind all this coaching stuff, just tell me what to do please!'

Some of the key skills you will need to develop as a coach are questioning, observing and listening – and then repeating the process. Coaching allows a person to think for themselves. The coach acts as a good sounding board to bounce ideas off. So why not develop your own coaching skills and coach yourself towards your personal objectives? To help you do this, you could use a well known technique called the GROW model.

The model looks like this:

**G**oals     –     Objectives (What do you want to achieve?)
**R**eality    –     What is the reality now? What is happening?
**O**ptions   –     Open to you (How many are there?)
**W**hat      –     Action do you need to take/Which option do you prefer?

When you get to the Slope of Achievement analysis in Chapter 14, you could usefully adopt the GROW model to overcome barriers. Coach yourself towards your success.

## Self coaching

So who needs to self-coach? Perhaps you don't have the opportunity to have your own coach, so putting your own skills into practice could be the next best option.

You have probably experienced a set of circumstances or situations where you felt it might be difficult to adopt appropriate behaviour, for example, that large business presentation, mingling at a conference, even socialising at a dinner party.

Think back to our advice about acting confidently in the previous chapter. Think of a positive role model and 'borrow' the qualities you need. Children are naturals at this – for example, they are excellent at mimicking sports personalities. When they are about to play a game of football, you will often hear them saying, 'I'll be Michael Owen.' Watch them play the entire game pretending to be that person, copying every tackle, twist and turn to perfection. Very few play the game as themselves.

Developing and coaching yourself to operate like a finely tuned engine will be essential if you want all the parts to work. It is easy to find yourself out of tune at different stages in your life for one reason or another. Frequent use of the GROW model on some of your smaller objectives can give you immediate success with a number of quick hits. If you imagine the pendulum on a clock, small adjustments at the top have a huge impact on the bottom and how far the pendulum swings.

Never underestimate the impact that small achievements have on your ability to be self-motivated.

Practising the skills of coaching will be like anything we learn in life. It means stepping outside your comfort zone and trying new things, being persistent and not giving up. It might feel uncomfortable to start with, but with sufficient time, practice and reinforcement, a new comfort zone is found for yourself to work within. Of course – like any new skill – it will take time to master.

Motivation comes from recognition and achievement. It is something that we want to experience throughout our lives. You may have an instance in mind when you were extremely motivated about something. What exactly was it? What did you feel like? You need to capture this feeling and store it away in a corner of your mind, because there will be times when nothing is working and your motivation is low. That will be exactly the time when you can re-open this corner and re-energise yourself with the feeling you had when everything was going well.

You will need a trigger point to recall the feeling at will, a touch, a word; anything that you can use as a trigger to re-open that corner. Again, this technique is used extensively in the sporting world. A well-known female tennis star liked to slap her calf to re-live and revive success.

It is often the way that once you or your team achieve that first success motivation is high and the winning streak continues. There are times when – once the first sale is made – follow-on sales start to flood in. Knowing what will motivate you towards success will be vital.

**Review and work plan**

1. Use the GROW model to coach yourself when overcoming barriers to success.
2. Coach yourself through difficult situations by modelling yourself on those that can do it.
3. Decide what motivates you.
4. Give yourself simple rewards.
5. Remember, small activities can have a huge impact.
6. Be prepared to step out of your comfort zone and work at it.
7. Concentrate on a time when you were motivated and look for a way to re-call that motivated feeling.

# CHAPTER 9

# *Virtual team-building*

> Nobody ever said you had to be alone on your path to success.
> Loneliness is a potential state, not a guaranteed one. You may
> decide to work in a partnership or with a team. Your team may
> be real or virtual, depending on your preferences. Real team-
> building techniques will be dealt with in a later chapter.

## Imaginary friend

The advantage with virtual team-building is that you can hire
and fire at will. Your team can come from any walk of life, from
the ranks of the present or from history, and not one of them
will demand a redundancy package if you decide they're not
pulling their weight!

Before you get sold on a virtual team, though, let's work out
the pros and cons.

Real teams or partnerships can also enhance your success
journey, although handling them may be more difficult.

Virtual teams need no such persuading. They come as part of
a fantasy package and – as such – are there to enhance and assist,
rather than resist and dissent. This is the type of team that you
create in your imagination, and yet their involvement and use
can make a real contribution to your success.

When you tackle a problem or rise to a challenge you tend to respond according to what has almost become a pre-programmed pattern. Most of this is down to learned behaviour and personality types.

These behaviours and traditional responses can help you in a situation, but in many cases their very narrowness can leave you at a disadvantage. Have you, for instance, ever admired a colleague's patience or sense of logic in a situation and come away wishing you were more like them?

Perhaps they have qualities you would prefer to draw on at certain times only. For example, you may admire their courage and daring in speaking up against the MD during a difficult meeting, but feel it caused them problems during a confrontation with a client.

By planning your own virtual team you can draw on famous strengths and behavioural styles at will, closing them down when they are inappropriate. The technique is simple, although it will take you time to practise.

Imagine you are creating your own fantasy football team to beat any world team currently playing. You can choose from any player, young or old, dead or alive. How would you go about choosing your team? You'd pick the best player to bring the greatest talent and strength to each position, weighing up the current situation regarding the opposing team.

In choosing your virtual team to help you achieve your own goals and success you are doing almost the same thing, only the strengths of the people you are going to select will probably be cerebral, rather than physical.

You will study your personal strengths and then any potential weaknesses. What areas need shoring up? Where are you most likely to be found wanting? Once you have discovered this you can begin to compile your virtual team.

If you were able to invite half a dozen characters to help you meet your challenge, who would they be? Each character may be selected for a different reason and each may be chosen for just one strength, rather than their total character. For the purposes of compiling your team you can include positives and exclude or ignore weaknesses at will.

Each member of the team is going to provide a voice on specific occasions for specific reasons. For instance, you may think you lack a sense of focus and determination when it comes to winning. Therefore you may decide to have Ian Botham on your team. You may want Winston Churchill there for his steely resolve. Perhaps you would like Eddie Izzard's sense of fun?

These are just guidelines. The team you compile will be personally chosen. You might find you want to include relatives, colleagues or friends in there. As long as they have qualities you feel you need then go ahead. Sometimes old schoolteachers emerge from the mists of time and take a place. You may have hated their guts but there was one quality that you grudgingly admired. Or perhaps there was an uncle whose advice you always cherished, or a grandmother who kept calm in moments of panic?

A bad team manager will pick sycophants. You are looking for people who will inspire and drive. People who will push you on, not people who tell you how overworked you are and to take it easy.

So what is the use of this virtual team? Put simply, you are going to seek out their advice when the going gets tough. How much use can an imaginary group be? Well, probably a lot of use. You know these people or you know their qualities. Most of their abilities will be yours as well, but – by hearing the words and suggestions come through them – you will have found a way to tap far further into your own potential.

What you will do by listening to the views of your team is bypass your normal thinking and behaviour patterns.

Very few people give us advice that we couldn't have given ourselves. All you are doing here is tapping more freely into that pool. For instance – imagine you have given yourself a heavy workload with tight schedules and deadlines in your quest for success. You may find you become fearful of the effort. You may hear your own voice starting to tell you that you have bitten off more than you can chew, or that you can't handle the pressure. Step forward Churchill. Listen to his view on the subject.

Or perhaps you start to believe that you lack the physical stamina for your task, that your goal is beyond your grasp? Then you might tap into advice from Mohammed Ali, or even Chris Moon, who lost an arm and a leg in a landmine explosion but went on to take part in the hardest marathon in the world. What advice do you think they might give?

Virtual team-building is a wonderful and creative way to use the power of your own mind. The characters you use may even come from fiction, if you feel they will contribute. If you are a Star Trek fan you may want Jean-luc Picard on board, for all his leadership skills. Or maybe Richard Branson, from the real world, for his entrepreneurial flair. Mo Mowlam could be there for her down-to-earth negotiating style, or even Bill Clinton, for his ability to bounce back in the face of adversity.

Posing a challenge to your virtual team will mean you get to hear a plethora of coaching voices. Visualising them all can be hard at first, but what begins as a relaxing and intriguing game can turn into a powerful technique for harnessing the power of your own mind.

Before you start you should build your team on paper, remembering that they can be changed according to circumstances.

## Virtual team players

1. My personal strengths

   ........................................................................................
   ........................................................................................
   ........................................................................................
   ........................................................................................

2. Weaknesses

   ........................................................................................
   ........................................................................................
   ........................................................................................
   ........................................................................................

3. Team member

   ........................................................................................
   ........................................................................................
   ........................................................................................
   ........................................................................................

4. Strengths they will bring

......................................................................................

......................................................................................

......................................................................................

......................................................................................

---

### Work plan and review

1. Create your own 'virtual team' to help creativity, brain-storming and confidence-boosting.
2. Use team members that will bolster your own personality weaknesses.
3. Be prepared to make team changes depending on circumstances and decisions.

# CHAPTER 10

# Team selection & development

> **Teams**
> Real teams are also potentially vital to your achievements, and you may need to build a solid team around you on your path towards success.

Successful people usually surround themselves with the people and skills that will enable them to achieve their aims and objectives. It's all about clarifying objectives and ensuring that you have engaged the necessary skills in the shape of the people around you.

It is a fact that many successful people don't have all the skills they need to achieve their goals, indeed many successful people have only *one* skill, which is how to be successful. However, they do have the ability to examine their task/objective, and then think about the contribution they can make themselves, and how others can help too.

Good leaders of people are often good because they clarify the task in their mind, develop a skilled team of committed people around them, and ensure that each individual is motivated with a clear sense of purpose and understanding about the role they must play. You must clarify your objective, be it large or small, and then decide who or what you will need to help you achieve it.

It is all too easy to team up with like-minded people with similar skills, but what you might be missing is a first-rate planner, or someone with greater persuasive skills. A group of similar people does not necessarily make a good team. Successful people have a great knack of identifying what is missing and then going out and finding it.

It is also about working with people that stimulate you and give you the greatest rewards. Successful people surround themselves with other successful people with similar values.

We recently listened to a tape by the poet David Whyte who talks about a swan out of water and how cumbersome it looks, but how slowly, as the swan enters the water, it becomes more graceful, agile and satisfied with its surroundings. Being surrounded by people and situations that meet with your requirements is important for you to gain satisfaction with yourself.

Think about yourself as if you were selecting yourself for the team. What is it you like or dislike, what might be missing, what would you change? Play to your strengths and pull other strengths around you in a variety of forms.

Successful leaders build successful teams to achieve a common purpose. To achieve anything in life single-handed is almost impossible. Don Wales, grandson of Sir Malcolm Campbell, needed a designer and a sponsor to build the car to achieve his dream – to break the land speed record – though he alone would be driving.

It can be all too easy to be single-minded and expect too much from your personal skills bank to achieve your goals, instead of engaging other people around you. How often have you attempted something single-handed when different skills were required from another quarter?

It is becoming more important for people to have the ability to work as part of a team. The strength of a team is usually greater than any one individual, so to achieve your objectives list the sort of people you might wish to engage and why.

Team member                    What specific task?

1.  ...................................        ......................................
    ...................................        ......................................
    ...................................        ......................................
    ...................................        ......................................
    ...................................        ......................................

2.  ...................................        ......................................
    ...................................        ......................................
    ...................................        ......................................
    ...................................        ......................................
    ...................................        ......................................

3.  ...................................        ......................................
    ...................................        ......................................
    ...................................        ......................................
    ...................................        ......................................
    ...................................        ......................................

4.  ...................................        ......................................
    ...................................        ......................................
    ...................................        ......................................
    ...................................        ......................................
    ...................................        ......................................

5.  ...................................        ......................................
    ...................................        ......................................
    ...................................        ......................................
    ...................................        ......................................
    ...................................        ......................................

Imagine your objective was to set up your own company. You
would need to ask yourself a number of questions and address
various issues.

1. What skills do I have?

..............................................................................

..............................................................................

..............................................................................

..............................................................................

..............................................................................

..............................................................................

2. What additional skills or advice do I need from others?

..............................................................................

..............................................................................

..............................................................................

..............................................................................

..............................................................................

..............................................................................

3. Financial advice

..............................................................................

..............................................................................

..............................................................................

..............................................................................

..............................................................................

..............................................................................

4. Banking advice

..............................................................................

..............................................................................

..............................................................................

..............................................................................

..............................................................................

..............................................................................

5. Marketing/Promotional advice

..............................................................................

..............................................................................

...............................................................................................
...............................................................................................
...............................................................................................
...............................................................................................

6. Legal advice

...............................................................................................
...............................................................................................
...............................................................................................
...............................................................................................
...............................................................................................
...............................................................................................

So having decided who you require to make up your team, it's now worth clarifying just what makes an effective team. The following page shows some of the key ingredients.

A team will only be as good as the person who leads it. When you develop your team for success, you should prepare for the stages of team development. Most teams go through several stages of this:

Forming  –  Storming  –  Norming  –  Performing

## Forming – stage 1

The group gathers together and meet each other. They will check each other out and make an initial assessment. Roles will be assessed and some information may be shared.

## Storming – stage 2

During the storming stage, competition for position will start. The team may attack each other or withdraw. Smaller groups with common interests may form. Each individual can have their own needs. The leadership may be challenged at this time, and this may be very uncomfortable for the group.

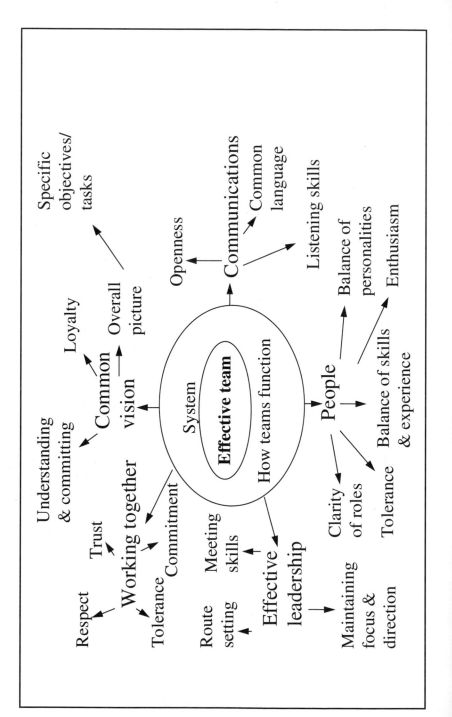

It is important to see this stage through, uncomfortable as it may seem, otherwise it will hinder cohesion and the feeling of togetherness. This stage is crucial for team members to come to terms with each other.

## Norming – stage 3

The group now agrees on a variety of ways of functioning, guiding their behaviour towards performance. Roles are clarified and individuals start to take responsibility for them.

## Performing – stage 4

Group members co-operate with each other to achieve the objectives of the group, working towards meeting the needs of each other. The group can focus around and harmonise with each other in the following areas:

| | |
|---|---|
| *Nurturing* | (Can help and inform each other) |
| *Energising* | (Plan, imagine and challenge) |
| *Performing* | (Carry out plans, implementing solutions) |
| *Relaxing* | (Celebrate and review, reflecting back) |

The group's needs and concern for the task are fulfilled.

Leading any team is a privilege and can be best described like that swan, insofar as you can glide on the surface but you will need to paddle extremely fast underneath to keep afloat. Leaders must *know* something and that's down to their technical ability in the field they are working. They need to *do* something, which is about the actions they need to take. They also need to *be* something, which is about the values of the leader and putting those values into practice.

Your team will need to be flexible and thus today's team members may change frequently to meet ever changing objectives for the future. Being a good team member is an essential skill.

## Review and work plan

1. Clarify your objectives and decide what skills you are short of to achieve them.
2. Focus on the qualities that will develop an exacting team.
3. Teams go through stages of development. Examine which stage your team may be at.
4. Reflect on your leadership and management of the team.
5. Work at getting maximum involvement from the team by doing the right things.

# CHAPTER 11

# Creativity

'To continue after several rejections requires motivation and the will to succeed. Money is not the motivator. It's the encouragement from my wife and the encouraging letters from the organisations I approach.

'One day I will walk into a shop and see something I invented on the shelf.'

**Duncan Edwards, Quality Manager**

To achieve any objective you will need the ability to think creatively. Having the mindset to become an imaginative thinker is not easy, but it is a major success factor for you and others to achieve your objective.

Organisations often create a culture and structure of people who readily identify problems but cannot solve them, either because of lack of authority to make the changes, or simply because it's easier to whine to a manager or partner about problems that are preventing you from achieving your goal than taking control and ownership yourself to resolve the problem.

Some organisations don't lend themselves readily to creative thinkers and spend all their time stifling new employees' initiatives and ideas by making the decision-making process so complicated

that people give up before they even start. The usual stuff gets
trotted out: 'We've tried it before and it didn't work', or 'You're
paid to work, not think.'

## The ability to rest

The ability to use your mind effectively will depend on the amount
of stress you are under – as discussed earlier in the book – as stress
influences our thinking. The amount of rest you take will also play
an important part in your ability to think effectively.

*Mike writes*: 'I remember my shift-working days and the
difficulties of totalling production figures at the end of the 4 x
12 hour shifts of broken days and nights. With my body clock
operating in reverse and without sufficient sleep I was less alert
and less intelligent, resulting in poor decision-making.'

Research has shown that there are two types of sleep: Slow
Wave Deep Sleep, which forms a large portion of the night,
mixed with some periods of Rapid Eye Movement sleep. With
Rapid Eye Movement, dreams occur.

Many of the areas of sleep remain a mystery, however, Harvard
Medical School recently demonstrated that a good night's sleep
can improve certain mental skills by up to 40%. Sleep is not just
about rest and repair, but is essential for memory foundation and
learning. So inefficient sleep or erratic sleep patterns will affect
your performance. How many times have you wasted nights
considering a problem and the options, thinking about the next
day's work or that large presentation you're planning?

*Mike writes*: 'I can recall lying awake for the best part of the
night prior to the London Marathon, the very night that a good
night's sleep was essential. The effect on my time was devastating.'

Many major catastrophes have been linked to human errors
because of lack of proper rest, particularly by those in charge, who
were responsible for making key life-or-death decisions.

## Stating the obvious

The ability to be creative can also depend on whether you have
an inquisitive mind, always looking and thinking of different

options and new ways of doing things. Children have immense ability in this area, not only to state the obvious, but also to come up with a whole raft of options available. What is it in life that takes that away from us as we move into adulthood?

A recent television programme on animal behaviour showed a chimpanzee trying to reach a banana suspended from a piece of string. The large compound holding the chimp contained a number of objects: two different sized rectangular boxes and a single wooden stick. The chimp at first tried to jump for the banana, but soon realised it was too high to reach. Scratching its head it considered the options. The box looked good, however standing on the box still proved ineffective. Too short, the rectangular box was tried vertically for extra height; still too short. Not to be beaten, the chimp pondered and considered the second box. This was balanced on top of the first box and after several frustrating attempts and numerous falls the chimp found that both boxes still fell short of the target.

The final attempt involved both boxes balanced end to end and the wooden stick. With one large swipe the banana fell to the ground. The desire to achieve the objective engaged the thinking of the chimp to use all of the tools available in the compound. How often do you see the problem as being too difficult or complex, and not even see the boxes or the stick, closing down your mind to some of the options available?

You might say the chimp was given the options and the banana as food was a strong enough motivator to use all of them. Who knows? It is important that you work with the creative part of your brain, the part that, if you're not careful, becomes obsolete through lack of use during your life. Like lack of exercise, the less we take the more relaxed the muscle becomes, until finally it is rendered useless.

## The courage to believe

To be truly creative will mean that you must have the ability to take yourself into uncharted territory in search of something different. Creativity means having the ability to have courage, belief and trust in yourself, having the confidence to try new things out. Again, many of you might come up with new ideas but fail when it comes to trying them out or implementing them.

There will also be times when you will be more creative than others. Get to know what works for you as far as your body clock goes. When do you function? When are you at your best? Is it early morning, mid-day or the evening?

As mentioned earlier in the book, brainstorming new ideas onto a sheet of paper can be an excellent way of allowing the mind to work in a less organised or methodical way. Some of the most bizarre ideas when first suggested often become the formula for a successful solution in the end.

## Stimulated by fear

Survival situations are often a good stimulant to creativity. How often have you listened to survivors talk about the creative ways they managed during life-threatening situations? How the brain managed to come up with a whole range of options to conquer the elements and help and support other people?

Sometimes desperate situations call for desperate measures and it can take this type of scenario to make you think in a lateral way. We are not suggesting for one minute that you create a desperate situation, but maybe from time to time you could operate as if the situation was a desperate one, if only to create the stimulus for response.

---

### Review and work plan
1. Develop your imagination to think about abstract ways of dealing with issues.
2. Look for the reasons why things *could* work instead of reasons why they could not.
3. Work under pressure and recognise your own stress indicators.
4. Ensure you get sufficient rest.
5. Have belief in yourself and trust your ideas – be confident.
6. Work at developing creativity techniques.

# CHAPTER 12

# The process of change

> Participation is about discussing what everyone else should do, involvement is about discussing what *we* should do and then going off and doing it.

Change is a part of life. As one door closes another door opens, or – as someone once said – 'As one door closes another slams in your face.' Therefore, you must consider the effect change has on you.

We often say that people don't like change, yet if that is the case then why do we change houses, room layouts and even partners? The answer is a simple one. You will be OK with change provided the change is controlled by one person, and that one person is you. It is therefore essential that you think about some of the changes you have been through, and how that was handled either by yourself or another person.

To achieve your goals, you will probably go through numerous changes. There are four key ingredients to think about:

1. Consider the change and who or what will be affected. Be clear about what it is you want, keeping your prime objective in focus.

2. You may need to consult others – those affected by any change – in most cases *prior* to deciding what it is you want to achieve. Consultation is a vital part when taking decisions.
3. You will need to be an effective communicator of the changes you intend to make, ensuring that everyone concerned fully understands the outcome.
4. Finally, you will have to check that the change has been made to your specifications, that is it working and, if not, whether you need to rethink your plan.

You will need to look at the four stages in detail and list your actions at each stage. Always consider the change and its effects on other people, as well as other situations that may arise from the change.

You will also need to create sufficient time to consider the implications of any changes that may occur when working towards your objective. This can be divided into two areas:

1. How the change may have an impact on your emotions, and
2. How that affects the way you function.

Remember how important your thought patterns are, their link to your feelings and, ultimately, your behaviour. Most of you will underestimate the power your thought patterns have on how you feel and eventually how you behave. If you think positively you will feel positive and behave like a positive person, as previously discussed. Conversely, if you think negatively, you will feel negative and behave like a negative person. The Simple Triangle shows the effect your thoughts have on the way you function. (See Triangle diagram opposite.)

It is easy to go through life seeing things from a negative point of view. Managers can be a classic example of this when they walk around finding the things that people have done wrong, instead of focusing on the good points and then raising awareness of what to improve. Morale would be ten times higher and performance would improve with such an approach. If you apply this logic to change, you can see change as a key opportunity to improve a situation, not as a hurdle to overcome.

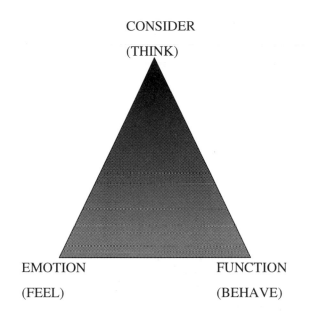

CONSIDER
(THINK)

EMOTION                    FUNCTION

(FEEL)                     (BEHAVE)

Probably the best mindset for change is to see it as an opportunity, not a barrier or problem. Again, another good example would be when a key person leaves the team, the manager can either view this as a skills and personality loss or an opportunity to review and restructure the team for better performance. Seeing change as an opportunity to improve is a mindset you can create by telling yourself that life is all about change, so if you accept this as a fact, you will not see it as something thrust upon you – though this will also depend upon the circumstances and how you are feeling at the time.

You may find coping with change easy or difficult, so when implementing change do so at a pace to suit yourself and the situation you find yourself in. Take marathon runners, for example, who increase the pace based on how they are feeling and the conditions around them. How many marathon runners burn out before the end because they set off too fast and fail to change their pace according to how they feel at particular times, only to be caught and beaten by a group who had properly paced themselves? You can only feel sorry for the person out in front when, after making a brave run, they eventually get caught and overtaken.

Getting to understand your feelings about change is an essential part of knowing yourself. Write down two lines about how you felt during your last experience of change and why this feeling occurred.

1.  What was the situation? ...................................................

    ..........................................................................

2.  How did I feel? ............................................................

    ..........................................................................

3.  What caused this feeling? ...............................................

    ..........................................................................

4.  What could I have done differently? ...............................

    ..........................................................................


As previously discussed, we are good at evaluating failure but rarely success. Teach yourself to evaluate what is going well, and why. Building on positive events is far more motivating than evaluating what has gone wrong. Evaluate successful change and why that was. Capture that feeling and store it away for the next change in situation or circumstances.

Seeing and accepting change is a key factor for a successful lifestyle. For organisations to be successful in the future they will need to recruit people who thrive on constant change, accepting and contributing at every opportunity.

Change can be less daunting than you think. You will, no doubt, have dreaded some change imposed on you, only to discover that once it had been implemented it was not as bad as you first thought. Why did you lose those countless nights of sleep, wasting energy through negative thinking?

As previously mentioned, the uncertainty of change can be hugely stressful. To quote David Lloyd George: 'Don't be afraid to take a big step when one is indicated. You cannot cross a chasm in two small steps.' This may or may not be the case, only you will know.

The next two pages show the stages of change. You alone will know what works for you.

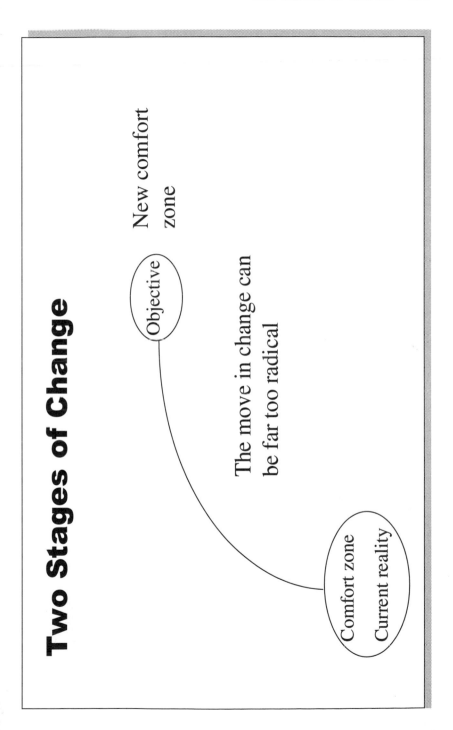

# Two Stages of Change

Objective

New comfort zone

The move in change can be far too radical

Comfort zone
Current reality

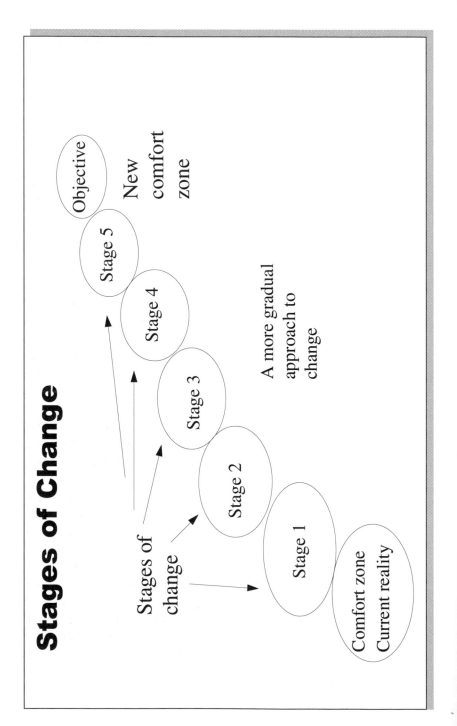

Change will mean that you will have to trust your decisions, and trust is about having the courage to commit to something without knowing the outcome. We can all make decisions when we are assured a safe result, with no risk involved. But life is a balance of safe situations and taking some risks. Think about the last risk you took and how you felt.

Your ability to trust anything in life will be affected by previous experiences and mistakes, yet without making mistakes you will never learn. As mentioned earlier, our learning and development comes from making mistakes. If we take no risks we play safe, with no mistakes – and probably no progress. How many millionaires have had failed businesses and yet made a complete comeback from bankruptcy to end up successful in another venture?

To be adaptable and resolute to change it is important to build self-awareness. 'What if?' is always a good question to ask yourself. Learning about yourself in these situations is important, increasing your knowledge and skill is vital.

The key ingredient for success will be your attitude towards the changing situation, and attitude can be further broken down into behaviour and confidence. The less confidence you feel with the change, the more likely you are to behave defensively.

Have you ever changed a situation and hated it? Have you ever encountered that awful gut feeling that – however much you tell your brain 'This is good' – your stomach tells you something else?

*Mike writes*: 'I remember once moving house to another part of the country for a new job only to find that I hated the place and the job. Even after years of trying to make it work there was a realisation that – if it took this much effort – it wasn't worth it. Maybe I should have quit sooner.'

We talked to one chief executive about approaches to change and he made a interesting suggestion: if there is no reason to change invent a reason as a catalyst to force other people into accepting it. The realisation that change is important allows people to examine what they are really doing and forces the mind into change mode.

**Review and work plan**

1. Develop a positive attitude towards change, see change as an opportunity to improve.
2. List the motivational factors that will carry you through periods of change.
3. Don't wait until change is imposed on you. Adopt a pro-active approach.
4. Take change in bite size chunks, unless you feel you can cope with one gigantic leap.
5. Assess the risk elements during periods of change.
6. If you are in a static situation then invent a reason to change things.

## CHAPTER 13

# Negotiating towards your objective

> **On negotiating**
> 'Negotiation is about meeting to seek agreement – not to win or lose.
>
> 'There is no point in turning up in your tennis whites debating the rules of tennis, when the other party is wearing American football gear.'
>
> **Frank Allen – National Officer, Institute of Professionals, Managers and Specialists**

In order to reach your objective you will sometimes need to negotiate. Negotiating is about discussing something in order to reach agreement and involves a degree of bargaining with the person or persons you are negotiating with.

Working towards a win/win situation is the ideal, and it is often easily achieved due to the fact that there is a line struck between your maximum and minimum objective and the other person's needs.

## Break-down

Negotiations often break down due to poor communication.

*Mike writes*: 'I can remember several employee sit-ins during my engineering days that were due to a failure to communicate honestly on some very minor issues. What is interesting is one fact: that at some stage agreement is always made, usually after a costly period of time for everyone concerned.

'It is important to understand that you must be clear about your objective, have more than one objective, and know your minimum acceptance level against that objective.'

## Bartering

Negotiation is not just about haggling over the price of something, but could be a whole range of things from the way something is done, to what you are trying to achieve and getting others to agree on.

Children are probably the best negotiators, mainly because they know exactly what it is they want and are determined to get whatever it is they are bargaining for. When you say 'no' they come up with an alternative response, followed by a second, third and even fourth reason for doing it.

If a child asks for a large ice cream and you refuse, they will often settle for a medium sized one or even a small one, usually with the fallback position of a lollipop. The child will eventually walk away with something, and usually it isn't too far from what they wanted. Children persist, and over a long or short period of time negotiate and eventually wear you down until you agree on something.

## Dog dealing

*Mike writes*: 'In my younger days when my parents responded by saying "We'll think about it" or "We'll see" it usually meant I'd won and would get what I wanted.

'I can remember negotiating to get a dog over a six-month period of time. My negotiations started with the key objector – my dad – who disliked dogs immensely and stated bluntly that he would leave before a dog came into the house. What a challenge! In my mind I realised that to convince him would be an almost impossible task. What spurred me on was the fact that

I desperately wanted one. It was at that time my only objective, to own a dog.

'Over time I developed a strategy which was to see how many other members of the family disliked dogs. After several conversations with my mum and grandparents, who lived with us at the time, I discovered they all liked dogs and the things they disliked were not even problem issues. I was motivated to a higher degree when I managed to negotiate money out of my sister for what we always called "her half of the dog". That piece of negotiation was always a mystery to me, because whenever the dog wanted feeding it was my half and whenever it needed walking or taking to the loo that was my half too! I eventually bought her half back, realising the difficulties with joint partnership and split assets at the age of nine.

## Patience and persistence

'Over a long period I continued to question my dad and discovered that picking the right moment was a key ingredient. I realised that after work when he was tired was not a good time to get a result, or when he had spent all evening at technical college, or was trying to fix the car or dig the garden.

'When I did pick the right moment – Saturday morning or after supper – I gleaned a huge amount of information from him and developed my skills of questioning, listening and remembering instantly. Over the given period he in fact told me an awful lot about what he disliked. By switching his dislikes to likes, I found that I could come up with a proposal.

'For instance, he didn't like big dogs, which meant he possibly liked small dogs. He also didn't like ones with long hair that would moult all over the house, which meant he liked ones with short coats that wouldn't moult. He also didn't like ones that barked a lot – the most difficult – but I did realise that some dogs barked less than others and I could overcome that one by training it not to bark by giving it extra food for being good. So I eventually came up with an acceptable specification:

A small dog
With a short coat
That wouldn't bark very much.

'His final objection was that he would not be walking it, particularly on wet winter mornings when it would be cold and dark. This I felt was a small price to pay for me to get my dog. I waited and at the right time eventually got him to agree. He realised he was the only one in the entire family who didn't want one and he caved in under group pressure from myself and everyone else in the family.

'His conditions were that I should walk the dog and feed it every day, no problem, with my second objective fixed in my mind – a larger dog next time. I agreed and honoured the proposal every day. I've had a dog ever since and now realise the power of bargaining, and how not to quit at the first obstacle.

'Reflecting back and using that story as a negotiating tactic: I knew exactly what I wanted, I was flexible enough not to be put off by the words "No, you can't have one", I was patient and developed a strategy to match what he wanted to reach agreement. I developed questioning and listening skills, coupled with patience and timing. Consulting everyone else was also extremely shrewd because winning their support strengthened my case in overcoming the barriers that he threw up against me. They also gave me other clues as to how to persuade him, such as approach times, when to ask and when to let it drop. This story took someone with a definite "no" stance, and through the power of persuasion and negotiation turned it into a "yes". Somewhere along the way there was a turning point that allowed the decision to change along with an element of face saving.

'Many negotiations fail because both parties do not want to be seen to be backing down, hence the deadlock. If you think back to some of the miners' strikes in the UK, both parties wanted people back at work, it was simply finding the solution acceptable. Producing the dog that met with my dad's specifications was my objective, because my bottom line was to get a dog, any dog, at any cost.

'I possibly could have taken him up on his first offer, which was to leave if a dog arrived, and saved myself the hassle. I did consider it, but realised there were other pitfalls. Having the ability to create that desire for something, the enthusiasm or determination, should not be difficult if you want something that badly. Negotiation simply becomes the key tool that allows you to get what you want as quickly as possible. I am sure you can think of a similar example during your life, where you have put your negotiating hat on and achieved success.'

## Creativity and confidence

To become a successful negotiator you will need the ability to keep an open mind, be creative, and have the ability and patience to persuade others. You must also have the ability to communicate what it is you want.

Confidence will also be a key ingredient. As you have already seen, confidence plays a major part in doing anything in life and lack of it can become the reason for holding you back. You might find that having the confidence to negotiate over the price or the condition of something is the only barrier to your success.

To negotiate effectively you will need to have a very clear understanding of the needs of the person you are negotiating with, by observing them and listening to what they are saying. You will also have to consider and agree in your mind a whole range of objectives and have the ability and common sense to be flexible about what you are trying to agree on. Many top level negotiations over the past years have failed because of the inflexibility and arrogance of both parties, with neither of them wishing to be seen as backing down. Leaving yourself a back door is important. Never negotiate yourself into a corner with nowhere to go.

It is also important to have something else in your back pocket, a trump card, so to speak. The greater your ability to explore all of the options and possibilities the greater your chance of success, so preparation is vital.

## Failing to prepare is preparing to fail

Engage in thorough preparation beforehand. You would get a poor result if you turned up for an examination or test without some prior preparation.

Brushing up on your communication skills will be essential, particularly when it comes to listening. It's likely you have not trained yourself to do this effectively. Your ability to prioritise inputs and outputs will be important if you are to become an effective negotiator.

The skill to reflect back what the other person is saying and feeling is important if you want to open the channels of communication with them. By reflecting back you are proving you have listened and understood their feelings about the subject.

## An exercise

A good listening and reflecting exercise to engage in is to sit down with someone and get them to talk about a subject that they feel strongly or emotionally about. Then use the reflecting technique to clarify your understanding of their feelings and emotions. Also, get them to feed back what were your key attributes as a listener – how did they know you were listening?

## Body language

Body language and eye contact also play a significant part. We communicate 55% of our message through visual means, 38% with the tone of our voice and a mere 7% by our words. This doesn't mean that you can say what you like as long as you have the right body language and tone. What it does mean is that if you use the correct words and communicate the wrong tone of voice and body language, then you lose the message. It would be a bit like telling someone you love them through clenched teeth. Have you ever had an apology with the words 'I'm sorry' communicated in a sarcastic manner and tone?

## Complex objectives

There is rarely one objective when it comes to negotiating. You might take a simple example, say buying some wood from a DIY store. You first have the purchase to make followed by cutting the wood into x number of strips to fit into your car. This may mean extra cost for cutting. You may also want the wood delivered to your home, and payment may be made by cash or credit card, all affecting the price of the job. Therefore, merely purchasing the wood may not be the sole objective.

Similarly, when you are offered a new job, salary is negotiable and so may be other benefits, like the car, the choice of medical cover, base location, flexibility of working hours, holidays, etc. These are a range of items to be negotiated as part of the total package. Be prepared to negotiate on each item separately.

## Investigation

Failing to prepare is preparing to fail, so fully understanding your objectives is essential. Therefore, getting information about the situation or the people you are negotiating with is important. Like most things this will take time, but it will be time well spent.

The more complex the situation or information you are planning to negotiate on, the more thought you will have to give to simplifying it. How many times have you found yourself in a negotiating situation confused by the information that you are faced with? The car salesperson who tries to bamboozle you with more information than you need and throws in low value interior mats and mud-flaps to make you feel you are getting a better deal? Keeping things simple is important if you wish to communicate effectively.

Our own negotiating skills were developed by observing how other successful people did it, picking up useful tips on the way. If you find negotiating difficult, repeat the confidence technique described earlier, i.e. list the things that make a good negotiator and become that person.

In preparing the negotiation you will need to consider your ideal route, the one you planned, but also bear in mind that negotiations may go down a different path, break down or take longer than you expected – possibly wasting a great deal of time and money.

*Mike writes*: 'During my negotiations to get a dog, time was of no importance so the six month period was irrelevant. I had all the time in the world, my opposition did not.'

## Squaring up

Assessing the situation in terms of who you are up against is vital. How experienced are they and/or are they the right people to negotiate with?

Considering the strengths (and weaknesses) of their case and understanding their objectives is also key. Much of your learning will be based on previous experiences and the sooner you can find that piece of common ground the sooner you can start to lay the foundation to build and work on.

The strategy you select and the tactics you adopt will be influenced by:

a) the issue you are negotiating on
b) your mood or state of mind
c) your values and your behaviour
d) the person or people you are negotiating with.

Always remember the importance of how you look in terms of dress or body language, and what signals they are sending to both you and the other party. Never limit your ability to manoeuver by making large or brash statements about what you are prepared to move on, or threats that would not be in your own interests to carry out.

*Mike writes:* 'Thinking back to my dad's statement at the outset: "If a dog comes into this household, I will leave", led to an enormous climb down on his part when eventually conceded. The statement was a brashly made threat that he had no intention of ever carrying out.'

Again, the timing and place for carrying out your negotiations will either help or hinder your success.

Making an attempt to pre-judge the other person's feelings will be another critical success factor. Consider how you can communicate effectively without the potential negative influence of any strong emotions you may be feeling at the time.

## Trade-offs

One good tip to remember is to gain agreement by trade-off, for example, 'I'll walk the dog if you feed it.' Children are good examples of this type of behaviour, e.g. 'I'll come shopping if you'll buy me a new toy', or 'I'll clean the car if you'll give me extra pocket money.' All great examples of trade-offs in return for something else.

*Mike writes*: 'I once worked on some very tricky negotiations. A finance director had acted out of procedure and clearly knew he was wrong. Half way through the negotiations we agreed to adjourn and decide on a different face-saving strategy with a number of off-the-record conversations taking place between myself and the other party. We quickly agreed and the solution was found with both parties concerned walking away feeling content with the outcome. The incident was over something trivial, and was caused by a breakdown in communication, management skills and policies.'

Remember, everything in life is negotiable, it's just for you to put into practice some simple skills to move you closer to your goals.

# POSITIVE WORDS

Master stroke

Favourable issues

Progression

Ovation

Triumph

Ascendancy

Advantage

Winning

Prowess

Checkmate

Fresh advance

Vantage

Prosperity

Feather in one's cap

Master

Feat

Walkover

## Review and work plan

1. Be clear about your objectives.
2. Clarify your acceptance levels – maximum and minimum.
3. Adopt a flexible approach where possible, look for a win/win.
4. Build your confidence and self-belief on every negotiation.
5. Always ensure you leave yourself a way out and keep something in your back pocket.
6. Fully prepare before any negotiations.
7. Develop the skills of questioning, listening and reflecting back.
8. Understand the person you are negotiating with and be clear about what they want.
9. Be prepared to walk away or adjourn the process.
10. Keep the negotiations as simple as possible.

# CHAPTER 14

# The slope of achievement

'The journey is as important as getting to the top; not just getting there, but how you get there.'

**Sir Chris Bonnington**

You are now going to make a start in producing your strategy for success by working through the Slope of Achievement analysis.

As discussed in earlier chapters, to achieve anything in life you must have an understanding of what it is you are trying to achieve. It sounds obvious, however, many people have no objectives at work or in their personal lives, but spend a great deal of their time questioning and asking themselves why other people are more successful than they are.

How often have you asked yourself: 'How did they do that, manage to get that job, afford that house, purchase that car, pull off that deal, or even look that good?' Often you convince yourself that maybe they were just lucky. Yes, there may be an element of luck to it, but these people have not just dreamt about it, they have stayed awake and turned the dream into reality.

The people who achieve things – either at work or in life generally – do so because they have a focus on what it is they are striving for, and are self motivated towards achieving their objective. The fact that they have this vision enables them to hone in on it clearly.

Whatever their objective, though, successful people are never 'trying' to achieve it, but are 'going' to achieve it. It's never 'if' I achieve it, but 'when' I achieve it. There is no question or doubt in their mind about failing because the desire to succeed is so strong that the thought of not doing so doesn't exist.

Have you ever wanted anything in life that much? Words like 'hope', 'possibly' or 'I'll try', don't feature. Have you ever told your children 'You'll never be able to do that', only to leave the door open for failure to be an accepted part of life?

We spoke to one school-leaver who had desperately wanted to be a marine biologist, only to be told by his teacher at school to go away and rethink because there was no way he could become that. De-motivation at its best. Do you accept similar advice, or look for ways of working towards your objective, even if it is just done to prove the other person wrong?

Not being influenced by other people's views is always difficult, particularly earlier on in life. You must have a clear focus on what it is you want to achieve.

Think about a time when you achieved something you thought was impossible, and how and why it happened. Did it come by chance? Were you merely lucky? Yes, maybe there was an element of luck. But the reality is you achieved your objective because you knew exactly what you wanted and were prepared to overcome all of those difficult situations or people who were up against you. The reality probably is that you got what you wanted against all the odds.

The desire to know what you want and to have the motivation to get it are two key areas. As previously discussed, it is important to create the time out from your busy day-to-day activities to clarify in your own mind what it is you want at work or in life. Remember, thinking time is important.

Achievement means something different to everyone. It is about what *you* want, not what society, parents or partners expect you to achieve.

We are sure you have achieved many great things during your life, yet find many things dismissed or undervalued because of the lack of recognition from those around you. Achievement is about recognising and reminding yourself constantly about some of those things you have achieved and continue to achieve. So there are a number of questions you should ask yourself. Refer back to your earlier brainstorming sessions.

1. What specific things do I want to achieve, either in my working life or my private life?
2. When do I want to achieve these things by? What is the deadline?
3. How difficult will this be for me to achieve? How steep is the slope that I will have to climb – the angle of difficulty?
4. What will be the barriers that may prevent me from achieving my objective? Who or what will stop me?
5. How will I overcome these barriers, by maneuvering around them or simply removing them?
6. How will I motivate myself along the way when the going gets tough and morale and motivation is low?
7. How will I recognise my success and the outcome along the way?
8. What is the current reality?

These are eight critical questions/considerations you will need to be working on during this chapter. These are explained in more detail below.

Once you have understood these critical questions, you can then work on the Slope of Achievement analysis to produce your personal strategy plan, both for your smaller and larger objectives.

## 1. What specific things do I want to achieve?

You may find that this stage is simple and obvious, and very little time will need to be spent on it. It might just allow you an opportunity to think, clarify and bring your objective into view, like picking up and looking through a pair of binoculars, adjusting the focus until a clear picture can be seen through both eyes.

However, you may find it is a case of creating time to think and reflect and take stock of the situation. Creating the time to do this has to be the first stage; not only creating the time, but the best thinking time for you, when you are without any of the stress that will influence your thought patterns and cloud your vision.

Think of a time when your thinking was at its worst and how difficult it was for you to see how to do the next job, let alone the job two stages away.

Thinking and reflecting don't always come naturally because we rarely take enough time to do them, usually because we are all far too busy with others tasks to allow sufficient time. Some successful people have said that they spend much of the time daydreaming and thinking about what they really want to do, creating that very clear picture in their minds. Managing your time will allow you to create this thinking time.

For some of you the view that you currently see is the one that you want, and that will stem from the contentment and motivation experienced from what you have achieved so far, with a desire to keep everything as it currently stands.

What is important for you to understand is that the focus and objective could change as you move towards it, as possibly a set of circumstances or simply a change in what you want could re-route your path towards another objective. So flexibility, stamina and patience will be crucial factors.

## 2. When do I want to achieve things by?

You will probably be used to working towards deadlines and the pressure that can be created from those time-scales. Pressure is good for you because it stimulates and gets the adrenalin going. Over or excess pressure, however, leads to stress, which is not good for you. As previously mentioned, stress can have dramatic and even fatal effects on individuals.

The deadlines or milestones that you set yourself need to be in harmony with you as an individual. The pace at which you work towards your objective will depend very much on how much time you feel you have. It might be about you having to break down your objective into short, medium and long-term goals, setting time-scales in turn against each one, bearing in mind that motivation comes from achievement. Each time you hit one of your milestones you will be spurred on towards your next objective.

The time-scale may be affected  by the situation and you will have to sort out in your mind exactly what is or isn't within your control. For your peace of mind, park those issues that are not within your control, enabling you to focus your attention on what is within your control instead of wasting time on issues you can have no impact on.

You may find this a dangerous process.  Many issues go into the 'out of my control' box as a sort of cop out. This is where you will need an honest and creative mind to allow you to think outside the norm.

The chapter on creativity will help you to think in a more abstract way.

## 3. How difficult will this be for me to achieve?

Many books and courses are developed in an attempt to create a mindset that you can achieve anything, provided you focus your mind on your objectives. However, it is a fact of life that to achieve anything worth having, there will be a degree of effort involved.

Again, an air of realism is important. It is quite possible that, having achieved your short or medium-term goal, you pause, break and reflect.

Chris Bonnington would not try to climb the highest mountain in the world in one attempt. Several camps would be set up along the route to rest, re-plan, communicate, reflect and discuss the challenges and risks – considering the next course of action before moving forward. If the conditions changed, moving forward might be impossible and the ultimate reality might be a complete  retreat and another attempt made at a later stage. It is important that this is not perceived as failure. Knowing when to quit is covered later in this book, because quitting might be the better option.

## 4. What will be the barriers I am up against?

Rarely in life do you achieve anything without some resistance, so it will be important that some thought and time is given to thinking about the type of resistance you are likely to encounter in working towards your objective. Ask yourself:

'What type of resistance will I be up against?'
'How will I feel?'
'How will this affect me?'
'How will I overcome these barriers?'

Many positive thinking programmes have failed because insufficient time was given to considering the obstacles, leading you to believe you could achieve anything, provided you focused. Many have found that motivation and morale have been hit hard at the first, second or even third obstacle, a little like a car running out of petrol and grinding to a halt, or a cyclist who has to stop on a steep gradient with no energy to continue. So unless preparation is made for the steep hill, it is likely to bring disaster.

A downward slope would help you enormously, allowing you to take your feet off the pedals, gather breath and energy, and cruise for a short period, or as long as the downhill slope lasts, which is hopefully forever. It would be nice during a mountain climb to find a gentle terrain with a plateau on it, or even to be able to plan the route with the plateau in mind.

It will be these barriers that will affect your motivation and morale, so it is important for you to understand what these two words mean (see step 6).

Barriers are likely to appear in a wide variety of forms and should be seen as opportunities to shape the route you take, not as a burden you have to carry.

Seeing potential barriers in a positive light enables you to create a different mindset, allowing you to take a new approach to overcoming them. Very few people go through life without any problems, so accepting that problems are a part of life is a good mindset. Seeing problems as opportunities or challenges to overcome is an excellent mindset to develop.

One of the greatest barriers might be the effect of your objectives on other people, and their response and reaction. Certain situations that affect you alone can be easier to cope with than those that affect others.

The barrier to success might be yourself, so structuring your thinking will be a critical factor in achieving your objective. We can often charge the self destruct button before we start.

## 5. How will I overcome these barriers?

Without clarity of thinking and flexibility you may end up like that unhappy hamster from Chapter 2, running endlessly around its wheel. Let's paint a more positive picture though. Go back to the hamster, but this time put him into one of those freewheeling plastic hamster-balls, going around the floor. You will notice that as soon as the ball becomes wedged against an obstruction, the hamster pushes against the obstacle, but quickly learns that no movement is made and steers the ball in a different direction, otherwise he will stay stuck in the same position.

It might be worthwhile making some movement when up against a barrier, rather than no movement at all. Small steps, if not large steps. Some progress is better than no progress at all.

You will need to develop a creative lateral mindset and think outside the norm to overcome some of the issues. You can often be drawn into tunnel vision and not see the passages leading out because your route is so fixed in your mind.

A good comparison would be a car journey. You look at where you are before you move off, and where you want to get to. On hitting some road works do you immediately look for an alternative route on the map or do you sit there and wait for the traffic to clear? Often there is not a route until one comes along later and a huge amount of time is wasted while you sit there. Another problem occurs if you find you have driven half the journey without remembering what you passed on the roadside, either because your focus on your destination was so strong, or because you were so pre-occupied with other issues that your mind blotted other things out.

You will need to consider all options available to you. Your thinking will need to be far reaching and creative. Work towards your best creative thinking time. Day or night your driving force towards your objective will need to be sufficiently strong to overcome any restraining forces.

In many cases a perceived barrier disappears or you find it never existed, except in your mind. Have you ever spent time putting off a dreaded phone call, only to find that it was not as big a hurdle as you expected, and end up asking yourself why you didn't do it straightaway instead of worrying yourself into a frenzy?

## 6. How will I motivate myself along the way?

Motivation is a wonderful thing and can stem from two areas – recognition and achievement. Taking these two areas separately it will be important that you have the ability to set stretching but realistic milestones so that you can feel this sense of achievement on working towards your objectives. Reflect on some of the measures you can put in place.

When it comes to recognition, developing the art of patting yourself on the back is a good one, giving yourself praise as if it was given to you by someone else whose words would give you a sense of personal value and worth. Think of someone whose praise would motivate you and imagine you received the praise from them.

One of the top five actions individuals require from leaders at work is praise and recognition for their achievement. You can create this self-recognition by awarding your own praise at each milestone.

Ask yourself the question: 'What motivates me?' We are all motivated by a variety of things. Write them down below. Use this as a tool to take you forward towards your objectives. Look for rewards that you recognise for achieving your objective.

You will need to work at retaining high morale. One excellent technique is to reflect back periodically on what you have achieved so far, creating a positive mindset to lift personal morale and motivate you towards your next objective.

List the top six things that motivate you in life:

1. ................................................................................................
   ................................................................................................
   ................................................................................................

2. ..................................................................................
..................................................................................
..................................................................................

3. ..................................................................................
..................................................................................
..................................................................................

4. ..................................................................................
..................................................................................
..................................................................................

5. ..................................................................................
..................................................................................
..................................................................................

6. ..................................................................................
..................................................................................
..................................................................................

## 7. How will I recognise my success?

Part of recognising your success involves being clear about how you intend measuring it. The link between achievement and motivation is the key. How many times have you achieved something trivial that you have put off for ages and then felt extremely motivated afterwards? Even simple tasks like sorting out the garden shed, mowing the lawn or putting up a shelf, once completed, can give a huge sense of pride and feeling of accomplishment.

Again, you will need to take time to focus on the smaller picture of success and the building blocks that will together make success for you. Each block will have a specific value in building your tower of success.

How often has your boss at work focused on the one thing that you did wrong and failed to recognise the 20,000 tasks you did right over the previous year? How many times have you walked out of an appraisal where the focus has been on what you *didn't* achieve instead of what you did? Your vision and thinking will need to focus on the achievements, recognising the perceived failures, but always cancelling and continuing towards your objectives. When Don Wales – the grandson of Sir Malcolm Campbell – failed to break the land speed record on Pendine Sands in South Wales, it would have been easy for him to focus on not achieving the objective. Instead it was seen as a first attempt with the objective of raising more sponsorship to make another attempt. Turning failure into a springboard for success is key.

## 8. What is the current reality?

Understanding and being realistic about your current situation will be essential before moving towards your objective. We have left this until the end because too often as human beings we get so bogged down and depressed with our current situation that our vision or goal seems unattainable.

By working back from your vision you will not fall into the trap of seeing the degree of difficulty at the start, and you will have begun to think positively about some of the problems you might encounter. That clarity of purpose will enable you to push aside some of the smaller issues that are holding you back. A good example to think about would be the purchase of a new house. It's the picture in your head of the new place that motivates you away from the arduous task of moving from where you are now towards your objective.

On examining the current reality there are three key attributes:

1. Be honest with yourself and others.
2. Be realistic about the situation.
3. Take action. Don't talk about doing something, get on with it.

Pretending something is not a problem won't make it go away. Remember, there will be many issues in your current reality that you like. Only too often people and organisations throw out the baby with the bath water for the sake of change. If it ain't broke, don't fix it, or break it for the sake of it, unless you find yourself on the treadmill or in a rut.

You should now have a better understanding of the eight critical questions, and their implications for you. You are now ready to complete the Slope of Achievement analysis, and chart your personal success strategy.

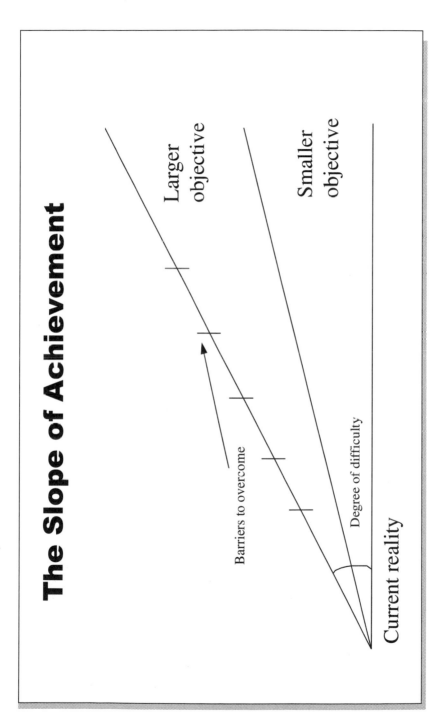

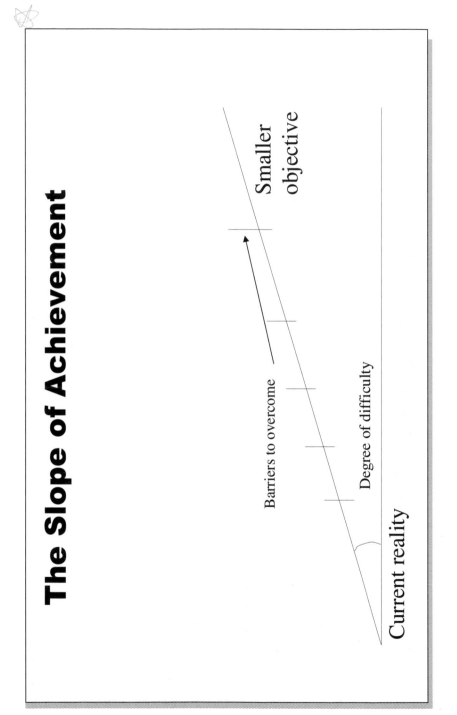

# Smaller Objective

| Visualisations | The now | Sustainability | Anticipation/ Preparation |
|---|---|---|---|
| What is my smaller objective? | What is the current reality? | What will motivate me? | What are the barriers to overcome? |
| Description | Description | 1.<br>2.<br>3.<br>4.<br>5.<br>6. | 1.<br>2.<br>3.<br>4.<br>5.<br>6. |

# Smaller Objective

## BARRIERS TO OVERCOME

1.
2.
3.
4.
5.
6.

## BARRIERS ACTION PLAN

1.
2.
3.
4.
5.
6.

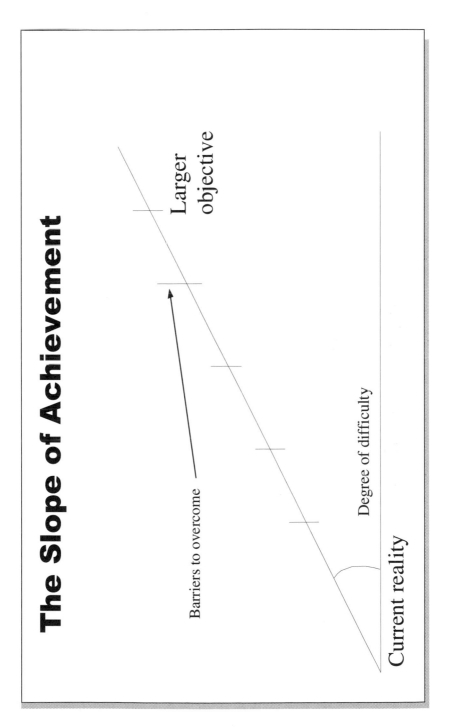

## Larger Objective

| Visualisations | The now | Sustainability | Anticipation/ Preparation |
|---|---|---|---|
| What is my larger objective? | What is the current reality? | What will motivate me? | What are the barriers to overcome? |
| Description | Description | 1. | 1. |
| | | 2. | 2. |
| | | 3. | 3. |
| | | 4. | 4. |
| | | 5. | 5. |
| | | 6. | 6. |

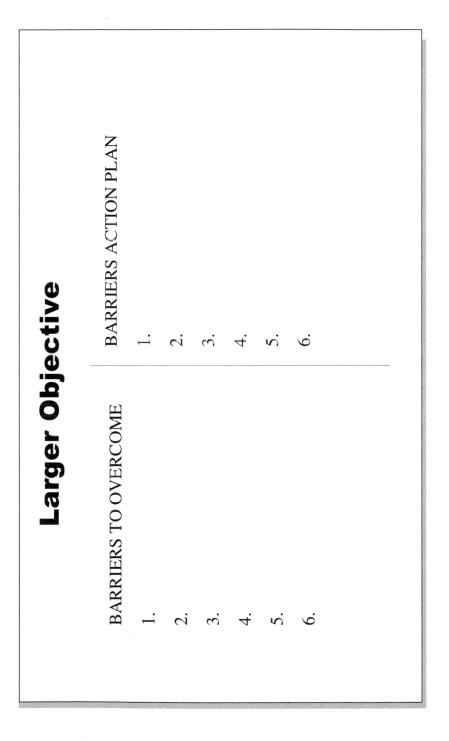

**Review and work plan**

1. Clarify your smaller and larger objectives. Be honest with yourself about the current reality.
2. Be clear and understand the degree of difficulty.
3. Understand the barriers you are up against and develop solutions to overcome them.
4. Set yourself clear milestones to measure your achievements.
5. Work on the things that motivate you.
6. Have a flexible plan, varying your approach if necessary.

# CHAPTER 15

# Prejudiced with ideas

'I attribute the success of the Morgan Motor Company to being honest to the marketplace and providing a car that is fun to drive and fun to look at.'

**Peter Morgan – Managing Director of the Morgan Motor Company**

*Prejudice*
'Appreciation of one's own identity and the other person's right to be different.'

**Huw Griffiths – Senior Lecturer on Social Work, University of Ulster**

Success is not just about winning and achieving your objectives, it is believing in the *right* course and achieving goals with ethics and integrity.

Achieving your objective is one thing, achieving it in a way that you are comfortable with is another. How many successful people can truly reflect back and be comfortable with the route they have taken in getting there?

*Mike writes:* 'I once won a fishing trophy as a junior angler. I remember the joy turning to sorrow when I thought a large weight used to bottom the keep net had been weighed in with the catch. The thought of winning unfairly took the euphoria and turned it into gloom and doom for the evening. I later found the weight in my fishing bag. It had not been weighed and the trophy was mine.

'When running my last London Marathon, it was not just about finishing, but making sure that I ran the complete distance as shown by the blue line on the road. For me, finishing was about making the complete run without stopping or walking. If I had stopped I would not have run the marathon, and would have felt unworthy of the medal.'

Success is not just about achievement, it is about how you achieve. It is not just about winning, it is about how you win.

Marathon running is an excellent example of mental strength and focus. When 27,000 people line up at Blackheath in London, the question they have in the back of their mind is: 'Can I finish? Will I beat my best time?' Even though the vast majority will have exceeded 20 miles in a straight training run, self doubt sets in: 'What if my laces open?' or 'What if I need to go to the loo?' are all energy-sapping negative thoughts prior to the start. You sniff a couple of times the week before the race and it instantly turns into flu, or so you think.

You will need to keep an open mind to succeed.

Keep an open mind about ideas put forward by other people. The next time you are at work observe what happens when ideas are raised – generally, our minds focus on why this particular idea will never work, with idea after idea being shot down. Of course, accepting any new idea contains an element of risk, and you should be aware of this, but don't close down possibilities too soon.

Your personal values will also influence how you achieve your goals. Take a few minutes to reflect and write down the things that you will hold as values in working towards your objectives.

Some might be as follows:

Co-operate values (company loyalties)
How you feel about it afterwards
Personal family values.

## Pain barrier

It is important that you consider the values you have listed and draw them as your bottom line. You may find that when you go below this imaginary line you feel some of the pain associated with failure and lowering your values. Failure to work towards and within these values can often create a whole new area of stress because your standards may have dropped.

Standards and values are something that only you as an individual can set. Of course, it may be an issue that is of no importance to you and that provided you reach your goals in life who cares what the effects have been in achieving your objectives. When Diego Maradonna punched the ball into the net and Brazil went on to win the World Cup, did the cost of cheating steal away the biggest prize in football or didn't it even matter to him?

Whatever your values, however, you will have to live with their consequences at the end of the day.

Prejudices are formed in a variety of ways: from experiences, the media, people and situations around you. You should be aware of this, and try to keep an open mind. Informed Scepticism can be a useful attitude to adopt…

## Informed scepticism

So what exactly is Informed Scepticism? According to Professor Huw Griffiths, Senior Lecturer at the University of Ulster, it will be one of the key business skills of the future. He describes it as: 'A skill, personal quality, value and knowledge base, demonstrating competency and understanding of complex issues. Competency is presumed to come from a "good enough" knowledge base upon which to base judgments. Informed Scepticism seeks to build on this benchmark quality.'

In plain terms it is an attitudinal skill (and therefore a trainable one) that seeks to probe, analyse and evaluate. It is an ability to look beyond the obvious and/or the superficial. It is predicated on a factual knowledge base that is free of prejudice. It is able to balance one set of competing demands with another. It is proactive rather than reactive. Informed Scepticism is a skill well worth cultivating.

**Review and work plan**

1. Keep an open mind. Don't allow the past to prejudice your thinking.
2. Remember, it's not about winning but how you win that's just as important.
3. Decide on a set of personal values and standards.

# CHAPTER **16**

# *Knowing when to quit*

> 'The expectations that other people have of you can affect and influence what you want in life for yourself. Knowing what I wanted enabled me to quit university to find happiness in doing something else. Knowing when to quit is important. The realisation that I was doing something because of the expectations that other people had of me made it a very difficult decision to take. Taking the decision to quit was one of my greatest achievements in life.'
>
> **Katherine – Customer Adviser**
>
> 'I don't think about the negative side of boxing, I just think about winning.'
>
> **Prince Naseem – Professional boxer**

Knowing when to quit can be an important factor in life. Sometimes having too much stamina and staying power can be turned into a weakness as an overdone strength. The situation can become dangerous if your risk assessment system doesn't allow you to realise it's time to quit. Only too often do we continue down a route or path telling ourselves 'This will work, I can make it work', instead of having the vision to recognise that we may need to take a different route altogether.

There is a fine balance between having the courage and

determination to achieve your objective, and the skill and ability to recognise that enough is enough.

You must also take into account how you may be influenced by other people, taking care that their well meant advice doesn't impair your ability to make a decision for yourself.

Knowing when to quit in the sporting world can often be a difficult decision, particularly if you are performing well and achieving your objectives. The decision then is more about whether to continue until you start under-performing or retire at your peak. Very often injuries play a key part and many athletes and sporting celebrities find themselves retiring due to the consistency of their injuries. As they overcome one problem they are hit by the next one, eventually deciding that their body has had enough and it's time to pack it in – not an easy decision to make.

*Mike writes*: 'In my teens I achieved the Duke of Edinburgh Gold Award, finishing the expedition over the four day period with serious signs of exposure due to the bad weather and the flu. Completing the expedition was very important to me. The pressure was enormous as one other individual had dropped out after the first 20 miles, leaving just three in the party. Had I dropped out of the expedition the others, for safety reasons, could not have continued.

'With seriously blistered feet, signs of exposure and exhaustion, we completed the expedition. The desire to achieve the objective and not let the other team members down was far greater than my ability to assess my personal risk and health. Arguably, looking back, concern for my personal well-being should have enabled me to make a different decision which would have been to stop and abandon the expedition, not seeing it as a failure, but as an opportunity to rest, repair and prepare for a second attempt under better conditions. However, my decision to continue was based on two concerns:

1. Letting the other team members down.
2. Being seen as failing to achieve the last part of the award.'

Achieving anything after a long endurance will give you a huge sense of pride, however, there really are times when – as painful as it might seem – giving up can be a far more courageous thing to do. Now might be a good opportunity for you to reflect back and think about a time when you should have quit sooner and ask yourself why you continued.

This chapter is not about developing a quitter mindset, it is about ensuring that quitting on your objective might be the right decision for you to make, giving you time to re-think your journey and plan another route. It might be you are carrying on with the same job but continuing to complain about how much you dislike it, instead of quitting and looking for something that satisfies.

Quitting anything is about making a decision and – as previously mentioned – making decisions is about considering what options are available to you.

It is important that you can justify in your own mind your reasons for quitting (or not), and that should be enough for you. Career development is a good example. Deciding what position you are at within an organisation, and sticking at that level, may give you a better quality of life than vying for promotion or looking for a new, fast-track job. Perhaps the comfort zone is right for you to carry out your duties without constant pressure or stress, and there may be something in knowing who's who, where to go for help, when the budget needs to be completed by, what pleases your boss, your colleagues, etc.

Why drive yourself harder when you can have a better lifestyle? Maybe quality time out of work is more important to you, and you appreciate the stability of your job. Who's to say there's anything wrong with that? Again, it's about re-visiting your objectives and being clear on the current reality and how satisfied you are with it.

It's one thing settling for an easier life for yourself but it's unfair when your leadership has an impact on others within the organisation. So take care that your own ambitions don't impact too greatly on others around you. Difficult isn't it?

As mentioned earlier in the book, some of you will be satisfied with your lot and therefore the desire to move forward will be far less. Some of you will be motivated by the challenge and pressures of working towards an objective and will need this stimulus to continue. It can be said that the things in life that come easy are for some reason valued less, while the objects that you work for and sweat blood over are valued and become lifelong treasures.

If you are not happy with a situation then why not quit and find happiness elsewhere? Finding that stimulus to make the move to quit can be difficult. However, being in a position to see quitting as an option is important.

You may have been brought up with the mindset that conditions you to think that to quit is to fail, instead of justifying to yourself the logic of giving up. One of the most positive quotes we heard recently was:

'They haven't failed, they have simply found another way that doesn't work.'

Often the decision to continue stems from what society and other people's expectations of us are. The endless bandwagon that makes you feel you have to conform with everyone else and their standards can scupper long-term success. You will only find success and happiness by jettisoning some of the things that, for whatever reason, are not bringing you the rewards you desire.

To quote Sir Chris Bonnington:

'When we finished the climb without reaching the summit, we weren't depressed by it.

'Failure is a necessary process to go through to get to the next step. It is an indulgence we allow ourselves, a set-back – you haven't succeeded this time, but there will be an opportunity to try again, along with an understanding that climbing has no written rules, which enables you to make them up for yourself. Of course, the risks are incredibly high, so knowing when to quit is vital given dangerous circumstances ahead.'

## Review and work plan

1. Know your limitations – be realistic about quitting.
2. Decide for yourself what you want and don't be influenced by other people and their expectations.
3. Consider all options open to you before quitting – how do you feel, how will you feel afterwards?
4. See failure as an opportunity to build the next attempt.
5. Keep your objective in mind. Know exactly what you want and why you want to achieve it.
6. Don't push yourself to the point where you put yourself at risk, physically or mentally.
7. Remember, often there are no written rules, it is for you to decide.

## CHAPTER 17

# *The summary*

The fact that you have picked this book up means that you have unachieved goals in your life.

The fact that you have read it, and used it as a workbook, means you are committed to turning those goals into reality.

You have an important choice to make now, though.

Did reading the book make you feel better? Did it in any way make you feel that you were moving in the right direction? Did it make you feel less guilty about doing nothing? And will closing the last page mean an end to your goal-focused efforts?

This book can be read and used in two different ways:

1. It can be used like a diet book. Diet books sell in their millions yet people continue to put on weight. Reading a diet book soothes their conscience by making them feel they are doing something. Especially as that 'something' requires minimum effort, short of flipping a few pages and – possibly – thinking.
2. It can be used to stimulate action. You will use it as a workbook for achievement.

Option two is better! The trouble is, the work is going to have to come from you. Knowledge is power, but only if it is converted into achievement.

Please use this book to make *yourself* rich/famous/happy/ successful, not us. Become that tall poppy.